AF662386

LIBRARY CLASSIFICATION AND CATALOGUING

LIBRARY CLASSIFICATION AND CATALOGUING

Modern Concepts & Practices

Anand Ballabh

AKANSHA PUBLISHING HOUSE
NEW DELHI • GUWAHATI • VISAKHAPATNAM

AKANSHA PUBLISHING HOUSE
4649-B/21, Ansari Road
Darya Ganj, New Delhi - 110 002
Ph.: 23263193 / 9811582579 / 09435116718
Fax: 011-23263193
Email: ektabooks@yahoo.com
www.akanshapublishinghouse.com

Library Classification And Cataloguing : Modern Concepts & Practices

© Author

First Published 2010
ISBN 978-81-8370-234-8

All rights reserved. No part of this publication may be reproduced or transmitted, in any form or by any means, without prior permission of the author. Any person who does any unauthorized act in relation to this publication may be liable to criminal prosecution and civil claims for damages.

[The responsibility for the facts stated, conclusions reached etc., is entirely that of the author. The publisher is not responsible for them, whatsoever.]

PRINTED IN INDIA

Published by Akansha Publishing House, New Delhi and Printed at **Harmain Offset Press**

Contents

PREFACE

"A vision with a task is dream;
A task without vision is drudgery;
A vision and a task is the hope of the world."

It is remarkable that classification and cataloguing are very important functions in the LIS management. In the present work an attempt is made to furnish latest information on modern concepts and practices in library classification and cataloguing.

Basically, Library classification forms part of the field of library and information science. It is a form of bibliographic classification (library classifications are used in library catalogs, while "bibliographic classification" also covers classification used in other kinds of bibliographic databases). It goes hand in hand with library (descriptive) cataloging under the rubric of *cataloging and classification,* sometimes grouped together as *technical services.* The library professional who engages in the process of cataloging and classifying library materials is called a *cataloger* or *catalog librarian.* Library classification systems are one of the two tools used to facilitate subject access. The other consists of alphabetical indexing languages.

Further, a library catalogue is a register of all bibliographic items found in a library or group of libraries, such as a network of libraries at several locations. A bibliographic item can be any information entity (e.g., books, computer files, graphics, cartographic materials, etc.), that is considered library material (e.g., a single novel in an anthology), or a group of library materials (e.g., a trilogy), or linked from the catalog (e.g., a webpage) as far as it is relevant to the catalog and to the users of the library.

Whereas card catalog was a familiar sight to library users for generations, but it has been effectively replaced by the online public access catalog (OPAC). Some still refer to the online catalog as a "card catalog." Some libraries with OPAC access still have card catalogs on site, but these are now strictly a secondary resource and are seldom updated. Many of the libraries that have retained their physical card catalog post a sign advising the last year that the card catalog was updated. Some libraries have eliminated their card catalog in favour of the OPAC for the purpose of saving space for other use, such as additional shelving.

This volume contains well-researched readings on different systems and practices in library classification and cataloguing. Other relevant issues are also suitably addressed. The following topics make core of the study—Library Classification; Cataloguing and Indexing; Automation of Library Operations; Classification in Practice; Cataloguing in Practice; Glossary; and Bibliography etc.

Definitely, the contents will enlighten and delight academics as well as professionals at various levels in the field of library and information science.

With the sole aim of furnishing authentic and latest information to the users of this book, we have tried our best by subscribing the views and works of different authorities in the field. Information is supported by facts and figures derived from various sources e.g. books, professional magazines and journals and relevant web sources. I express my gratitude to them all. While working on this project I was immensely benefitted by the guidance, assistance and inspiration extended by my seniors, colleagues and family members. I am grateful to them all. Finally, I am thankful to my publishers for undertaking publication of this book.

We will appreciate if the readers could communicate their comments and suggestions to make this more useful and informative, which we will incorporate in the subsequent eidition with due acknowledgement.

—AB

1

LIBRARY CLASSIFICATION

First, it is remarkable to note that by a library classification we mean a system of coding and organizing library materials (books, serials, audiovisual materials, computer files, maps, manuscripts, realia) according to their subject and allocating a call number to that information resource. Similar to classification systems used in biology, bibliographic classification systems group entities that are similar together typically arranged in a hierarchical tree structure. A different kind of classification system, called a faceted classification system, is also widely used which allows the assignment of multiple classifications to an object, enabling the classifications to be ordered in multiple manners.

Basically, Library classification forms part of the field of library and information science. It is a form of bibliographic classification (library classifications are used in library catalogs, while "bibliographic classification" also covers classification used in other kinds of bibliographic databases). It goes hand in hand with library (descriptive) cataloging under the rubric of *cataloging and classification,* sometimes grouped together as *technical services*. The library professional who engages in the process of cataloging and classifying library materials is called a *cataloger* or *catalog librarian*. Library classification systems are one of the two tools used to facilitate subject access. The other consists of alphabetical indexing languages such as Thesauri and Subject Headings systems.

Library classification of a piece of work consists of two steps. Firstly the "aboutness" of the material is ascertained. Next, a call number (essentially a book's address), based on the classification system in use at the particular library will be assigned to the work using the notation of the system.

It is important to note that unlike subject heading or thesauri where multiple terms can be assigned to the same work, in library classification systems, each work can only be placed in one class. This is due to shelving purposes: A book can have only one physical place. However in classified catalogs one may have main entries as well as added entries. Most classification systems like the Dewey Decimal Classification (DDC) and Library of Congress classification also add a cutter number to each work which adds a code for the author of the work.

Classification systems in libraries generally play two roles. Firstly they facilitate subject access by allowing the user to find out what works or documents the library has on a certain subject. Secondly, they provide a known location for the information source to be located (e.g where it is shelved).

Until the 19th century, most libraries had closed stacks, so the library classification only served to organize the subject catalog. In the 20th century, libraries opened their stacks to the public and started to shelve the library material itself according to some library classification to simplify subject browsing.

Some classification systems are more suitable for aiding subject access, rather than for shelf location. For example, UDC which uses a complicated notation including plus, colons are more difficult to use for the purpose of shelf arrangement but are more expressive compared to DDC in terms of showing relationships between subjects. Similarly faceted classification schemes are more difficult to use for shelf arrangement, unless the user has knowledge of the citation order.

Depending on the size of the library collection, some libraries might use classification systems solely for one purpose or the other. In extreme cases a public library with a small collection might just use a classification system for location of resources but might not use a complicated subject classification system. Instead all resources might just be put into a couple of wide classes (Travel, Crime, Magazines etc). This is known as a "mark and park" classification method, more formally called reader interest classification

Main Types

There are many standard system of library classification in use, and many more have been proposed over the years. However in general, Classification systems can be divided into three types depending on how they are used.

1. Universal schemes covering all subjects. Examples include Dewey Decimal Classification, Universal Decimal Classification and Library of Congress Classification
2. Specific classification schemes for particular subjects or types of materials. Examples include Iconclass, British Catalogue of Music Classification, and Dickinson classification, or the NLM Classification for medicine.
3. National schemes specially created for certain countries. An example is the Swedish library classification system, SAB (Sveriges Allmänna Biblioteksförening).

Further, in terms of functionality, classification systems are often described as

1. enumerative: produce an alphabetical list of subject headings, assign numbers to each heading in alphabetical order
2. hierarchical: divides subjects hierarchically, from most general to most specific
3. faceted or analytico-synthetic: divides subjects into mutually exclusive orthogonal facets

There are few completely enumerative systems or faceted systems, most systems are a blend but favouring one type or the other. The most common classification systems, LCC and DDC, are essentially enumerative, though with some hierarchical and faceted elements (more so for DDC), especially at the broadest and most general level. The first true faceted system was the Colon classification of Dr. S. R. Ranganathan.

Universal Classification Systems Used in English-Speaking World

- Bliss bibliographic classification (BC)
- Dewey Decimal Classification (DDC)
- Library of Congress Classification (LCC)
- Harvard-Yenching Classification: An English classification system for Chinese language materials.
- Open Shelves Classification: "a free, humble, modern, open-source, crowd-sourced replacement for the Dewey Decimal System."

Some of these systems are elaborately dealt with in this chapter.

Universal Classification Systems in Other Languages

- A System of Book Classification for Chinese Libraries (Liu's Classification)
    - o New Classification Scheme for Chinese Libraries
- Nippon Decimal Classification (NDC)
- Chinese Library Classification (CLC)
- Korean Decimal Classification (KDC)
- Library-Bibliographic Classification (BBK) from Russia.

Universal Classification Systems that Rely on Synthesis

- Bliss bibliographic classification
- Colon classification
- Cutter Expansive Classification
- Universal Decimal Classification

Newer classification systems tend to use the principle of synthesis (combining codes from different lists to represent the different attributes of a work) heavily, which is comparatively lacking in LC or DDC.

Main Differences

As a result of differences in Notation, history, use of enumeration, hierarchy, facets, classification systems can differ in the following ways

1. *Expressiveness:* This is the degree in which the notation can express relationship between concepts or structure.
2. *Type of Notation:* Notation can be pure (consisting of only numerals for example) or mixed (consisting of letters, numerals, and other symbols).
3. *Whether they support mnemonics:* For example the number 44 in DDC notation usually means it concerns

some aspect of France. For example 598.0944 concerns "Birds in France". the 09 signifies country code, and 44 represents France.

4. *Hospitality:* The degree in which the system is able to accommodates new subjects
5. Simplicity
6. Consistency
7. *Speed of updates and degree of support:* The best classification systems are constantly being reviewed and improved.
8. *Brevity:* Length of the notation to express the same concept

DEWEY DECIMAL CLASSIFICATION

The Dewey Decimal Classification (DDC, also called the Dewey Decimal System) is a proprietary system of library classification developed by Melvil Dewey in 1876, and has been greatly modified and expanded through 22 major revisions, the most recent in 2004. This system organizes books on library shelves in a specific and repeatable order that makes it easy to find any book and return it to its proper place.

The DDC attempts to organize all knowledge into ten main classes. The ten main classes are each further subdivided into ten divisions, and each division into ten sections, giving ten main classes, 100 divisions and 1000 sections. DDC's advantage in using decimals for its categories allows it to be both purely numerical and infinitely hierarchical.

It also uses some aspects of a faceted classification scheme, combining elements from different parts of the structure to construct a number representing the subject content (often combining two subject elements with linking numbers and geographical and temporal elements) and form of an item rather than drawing upon a list containing each class and its meaning. Except for general works and fiction, works are classified principally by subject, with extensions for subject relationships, place, time or type of material, producing classification numbers of at least three digits but otherwise of indeterminate length with a decimal point before the fourth digit, where present (e.g. 330 for economics + .9 for geographic treatment + .04 for Europe = 330.94 European economy; 973 for United States + .05 form division for periodicals = 973.05 periodicals concerning the United States generally).

In fact, Books are placed on the shelf in increasing numerical order of the decimal number, e.g. 050, 220, 330, 330.973, 331. When two books have the same classification number the second line of the call number (usually the first letter or letters of the author's last name, the title if there is no identifiable author) is placed in alphabetical order.

It is a common misconception that all books in the DDC are non-fiction. The DDC has a number for all books, including fiction: American fiction is classified in 813. Most libraries create a separate fiction section to allow shelving in a more generalized fashion than Dewey provides for, or to avoid the space that would be taken up in the 800s.

Some parts of the classification offer options which may be adopted by different kinds of libraries. An important feature of the scheme is the possibility of assigning multiple class numbers to a bibliographical item and only using one of them for the shelving. The added numbers will then be found in the classified subject catalog (though this is not the usual practice in North America). For the full benefit of the scheme the relative index and the tables which form part of every edition need to be understood and consulted when required. The structure of the schedules is such that subjects which would be close to each other in a dictionary catalog are those which are dispersed in the Dewey schedules (e.g. architecture of Chicago quite separate from geography of Chicago).

Classes Listed

The system is made up of ten main classes or categories, each divided into ten secondary classes or subcategories, each having ten subdivisions.

- 000 – Computer science, information & general works
- 100 – Philosophy and psychology
- 200 – Religion
- 300 – Social sciences
- 400 – Language
- 500 – Science (including mathematics)
- 600 – Technology
- 700 – Arts and recreation
- 800 – Literature
- 900 – History, geography, and biography

During his life time Melvil Dewey edited each edition himself: he was followed by other editors who had been very much influenced by him. The earlier editions were printed in the peculiar spelling that Dewey had devised: the number of volumes in each edition increased to two, then three and now four.

The Online Computer Library Center of Dublin, Ohio acquired the trademark and copyrights associated with the DDC when it bought Forest Press in 1988. OCLC maintains the classification system and publishes new editions of the system. The editorial staff responsible for updates is based partly at the Library of Congress and partly at OCLC. Their work is reviewed by the Decimal Classification Editorial Policy Committee (EPC), which is a ten-member international board that meets twice each year. The four-volume unabridged edition is published approximately every seven years, the most recent edition (DDC 22) in mid 2003. The web edition is updated on an ongoing basis, with changes announced each month.

The work of assigning a DDC number to each newly published book is performed by a division of the Library of Congress, whose recommended assignments are either accepted or rejected by the OCLC after review by an advisory board; to date all have been accepted.

It is pertinent to note here that, in September 2003, the OCLC sued the Library Hotel for trademark infringement. The settlement was that the OCLC would allow the Library Hotel to use the system in its hotel and marketing. In exchange, the Hotel would acknowledge the Center's ownership of the trademark and make a donation to a nonprofit organization promoting reading and literacy among children.

DDC's numbers formed the basis of the more expressive but complex Universal Decimal Classification (UDC), which combines the basic Dewey numbers with selected punctuation marks (comma, colon, parentheses, etc.). Adaptations of DDC for specific regions outside the English-speaking world include the Korean Decimal Classification, the New Classification Scheme for Chinese Libraries and the Nippon Decimal Classification (Japanese).

Besides its frequent revision, DDC's main advantage over its chief American rival, the Library of Congress Classification system developed shortly afterward, is its simplicity. Thanks to the use of pure notation, a mnemonics system and a hierarchical decimal place system, it is generally easier to use.

DDC and UDC are more flexible than Library of Congress Classification because of greater use of facets (via auxiliary tables) while Library of Congress Classification is almost totally enumerative.

DDC's decimal system means that it is less hospitable to the addition of new subjects, as opposed to Library of Congress Classification, which has 21 classes at the top level. DDC notations can be much longer compared to other classification systems.

One more disadvantage of DDC is that it was developed in the 19th century essentially by one man and was built on a top-down approach to classify all human knowledge, which makes it difficult to adapt to changing fields of knowledge. The Library of Congress Classification system was developed based mainly on the idea of literary warrant; classes were added (by individual experts in each area) only when needed for works owned by the Library of Congress. As a result, while the Library of Congress Classification system was able to incorporate changes and additions of new branches of knowledge, particularly in the fields of engineering and computer science (the greater hospitability of the Library of Congress Classification was also a factor), DDC has been criticized for being inadequate in covering those areas.

It is asserted that, as a result, most major academic libraries in the US do not use the DDC because the classification of works in those areas is not specific enough, although there are other reasons that may truly be more weighty, such as the much lower expense of using a unique "pre-packaged" catalog number instead of having highly skilled staff members engaging in the time-consuming development of catalog numbers.

The Library of Congress Classification system is not without problems. Because each area is developed by an expert according to demands of cataloging, there is little consistency. It is also highly US-centric (more so than DDC) because of the nature of the system, and it has been translated into far fewer languages than DDC and UDC.

Outline of Dewey Decimal classes

The Dewey Decimal Classification is a system of library classification made up of ten main classes or categories, each divided into ten secondary classes or subcategories, each having ten subdivisions. This system is a logical way of classifying a comprehensive array of disciplines, whether academic or practical.

Classes

000 – Computer Science, Information & General Works

- 000 Computer science, knowledge & systems
  - o 000 Computer science, information & general works
  - o 001 Knowledge
  - o 002 The book
  - o 003 Systems
  - o 004 Data processing & computer science
  - o 005 Computer programming, programs & data
  - o 006 Special computer methods
  - o 007 [Unassigned]
  - o 008 [Unassigned]
  - o 009 [Unassigned]

- 010 Bibliographies
  - o 010 Bibliography
  - o 011 Bibliographies
  - o 012 Bibliographies of individuals
  - o 013 [Unassigned]
  - o 014 Of anonymous & pseudonymous works
  - o 015 Bibliographies of works from specific places
  - o 016 Bibliographies of works on specific subjects
  - o 017 General subject catalogs
  - o 018 Catalogs arranged by author, date, etc.
  - o 019 Dictionary catalogs
- 020 Library & information sciences
  - o 020 Library & information sciences
  - o 021 Library relationships
  - o 022 Administration of physical plant
  - o 023 Personnel management
  - o 024 *No longer used — formerly Regulations for readers*
  - o 025 Library operations
  - o 026 Libraries for specific subjects
  - o 027 General libraries
  - o 028 Reading & use of other information media
  - o 029 No longer used — formerly Literary methods
- 030 Encyclopedias & books of facts
  - o 030 General encyclopedic works
  - o 031 Encyclopedias in American English
  - o 032 Encyclopedias in English

- 033 In other Germanic languages
- 034 Encyclopedias in French, Occitan & Catalan
- 035 In Italian, Romanian & related languages
- 036 Encyclopedias in Spanish & Portuguese
- 037 Encyclopedias in Slavic languages
- 038 Encyclopedias in Scandinavian languages
- 039 Encyclopedias in other languages

- 040 *No longer used — formerly Collected essays by language*
  - 040 [Unassigned]
  - 041 [Unassigned]
  - 042 [Unassigned]
  - 043 [Unassigned]
  - 044 [Unassigned]
  - 045 [Unassigned]
  - 046 [Unassigned]
  - 047 [Unassigned]
  - 048 [Unassigned]
  - 049 [Unassigned]
- 050 Magazines, journals & serials
  - 050 General serial publications
  - 051 Serials in American English
  - 052 Serials in English
  - 053 Serials in other Germanic languages
  - 054 Serials in French, Occitan & Catalan
  - 055 In Italian, Romanian & related languages
  - 056 Serials in Spanish & Portuguese
  - 057 Serials in Slavic languages

- 058 Serials in Scandinavian languages
- 059 Serials in other languages

- 060 Associations, organizations & museums
  - 060 General organizations & museum science
  - 061 Organizations in North America
  - 062 Organizations in British Isles; in England
  - 063 Organizations in central Europe; in Germany
  - 064 Organizations in France & Monaco
  - 065 Organizations in Italy & adjacent islands
  - 066 In Iberian Peninsula & adjacent islands
  - 067 Organizations in eastern Europe; in Russia
  - 068 Organizations in other geographic areas
  - 069 Museum science
- 070 News media, journalism & publishing
  - 070 News media, journalism & publishing
  - 071 Newspapers in North America
  - 072 Newspapers in British Isles; in England
  - 073 Newspapers in central Europe; in Germany
  - 074 Newspapers in France & Monaco
  - 075 Newspapers in Italy & adjacent islands
  - 076 In Iberian Peninsula & adjacent islands
  - 077 Newspapers in eastern Europe; in Russia
  - 078 Newspapers in Scandinavia
  - 079 Newspapers in other geographic areas
- 080 General collections
  - 080 General collections
  - 081 Collections in American English

  - o 082 Collections in English
  - o 083 Collections in other Germanic languages
  - o 084 Collections in French, Occitan & Catalan
  - o 085 In Italian, Romanian & related languages
  - o 086 Collections in Spanish & Portuguese
  - o 087 Collections in Slavic languages
  - o 088 Collections in Scandinavian languages
  - o 089 Collections in other languages
- 090 Manuscripts & rare books
  - o 090 Manuscripts & rare books
  - o 091 Manuscripts
  - o 092 Block books
  - o 093 Incunabula
  - o 094 Printed books
  - o 095 Books notable for bindings
  - o 096 Books notable for illustrations
  - o 097 Books notable for ownership or origin
  - o 098 Prohibited works, forgeries & hoaxes
  - o 099 Books notable for format

100 – Philosophy and Psychology

- 100 Philosophy & psychology
  - o 100 Philosophy & psychology
  - o 101 Theory of philosophy
  - o 102 Miscellany of philosophy
  - o 103 Dictionaries of philosophy
  - o *104 No longer used — formerly Essays*
  - o 105 Serial publications of philosophy

- 106 Organizations of philosophy
- 107 Education, research in philosophy
- 108 Kinds of persons in philosophy
- 109 Historical treatment of philosophy

- 110 Metaphysics
  - 110 Metaphysics
  - 111 Ontology
  - *112 No longer used — formerly Methodology*
  - 113 Cosmology (Philosophy of nature)
  - 114 Space
  - 115 Time
  - 116 Change
  - 117 Structure
  - 118 Force & Energy
  - 119 Number & quantity
- 120 Epistemology, causation, humankind
  - 120 Epistemology, causation & humankind
  - 121 Epistemology (Theory of knowledge)
  - 122 Causation
  - 123 Determinism & indeterminism
  - 124 Teleology
  - *125 No longer used — formerly Infinity*
  - 126 The self
  - 127 The unconscious & the subconscious
  - 128 Humankind
  - 129 Origin & destiny of individual souls
- 130 Paranormal phenomena

  - 130 Parapsychology & occultism
  - 131 Occult methods for achieving well-being
  - *132 No longer used — formerly Mental derangements*
  - 133 Parapsychology & occultism
  - *134 No longer used — fomerly Mesmerism and Clairvoyance*
  - 135 Dreams & mysteries
  - *136 No longer used — formerly Mental characteristics*
  - 137 Divinatory graphology
  - 138 Physiognomy
  - 139 Phrenology
- 140 Specific philosophical schools
  - 140 Specific philosophical schools
  - 141 Idealism & related systems
  - 142 Critical philosophy
  - 143 Intuitionism & Bergsonism
  - 144 Humanism & related systems
  - 145 Sensationalism
  - 146 Naturalism & related systems
  - 147 Pantheism & related systems
  - 148 Liberalism, eclecticism, traditionalism
  - 149 Other philosophical systems
- 150 Psychology
  - 150 Psychology
  - *151 No longer used — formerly Intellect*
  - 152 Perception, movement, emotions, drives
  - 153 Mental processes & intelligence

  - 154 Subconscious & altered states
  - 155 Differential & developmental psychology
  - 156 Comparative psychology
  - *157 No longer used — formerly Emotions*
  - 158 Applied psychology
  - *159 No longer used — formerly Will*
- 160 Logic
  - 160 Logic
  - 161 Induction
  - 162 Deduction
  - *163 Not assigned or no longer used*
  - *164 Not assigned or no longer used*
  - 165 Fallacies & sources of error
  - 166 Syllogisms
  - 167 Hypotheses
  - 168 Argument & persuasion
  - 169 Analogy
- 170 Ethics (Moral philosophy)
  - 170 Ethics
  - 171 Systems & doctrines
  - 172 Political ethics
  - 173 Ethics of family relationships
  - 174 Economic & professional ethics
  - 175 Ethics of recreation & leisure
  - 176 Ethics of sex & reproduction
  - 177 Ethics of social relations
  - 178 Ethics of consumption
  - 179 Other ethical norms

- 180 Ancient, medieval, Oriental philosophy
  - 180 Ancient, medieval & eastern philosophy
  - 181 Oriental philosophy
  - 182 Pre-Socratic Greek philosophies
  - 183 Sophistic & Socratic philosophies
  - 184 Platonic philosophy
  - 185 Aristotelian philosophy
  - 186 Skeptic and Neoplatonic philosophies
  - 187 Epicurean philosophy
  - 188 Stoic philosophy
  - 189 Medieval Western philosophy
- 190 Modern Western philosophy (19th-century, 20th-century)
  - 190 Modern western philosophy
  - 191 Modern Western philosophy United States & Canada
  - 192 Modern Western philosophy British Isles
  - 193 Modern Western philosophy Germany & Austria
  - 194 Modern Western philosophy France
  - 195 Modern Western philosophy Italy
  - 196 Modern Western philosophy Spain & Portugal
  - 197 Modern Western philosophy Soviet Union
  - 198 Modern Western philosophy Scandinavia
  - 199 Modern Western philosophy Other geographical areas

200 – Religion

- 200 Religion
  - 201 Religious mythology, general classes of religion, interreligious relations and attitudes, social theology
  - 202 Doctrines
  - 203 Public worship and other practices
  - 204 Religious experience, life, practice
  - 205 Religious ethics
  - 206 Leaders and organization
  - 207 Missions and religious education
  - 208 Sources
  - 209 Sects and reform movements
- 210 Natural theology
  - 211 Concepts of God
  - 212 Existence, attributes of God
  - 213 Creation
  - 214 Theodicy
  - 215 Science & religion
  - *216 No longer used – formerly Evil*
  - *217 No longer used – formerly Prayer*
  - 218 Humankind
  - *219 No longer used – formerly Analogies*
- 220 Bible
  - 221 Old Testament
  - 222 Historical books of Old Testament
  - 223 Poetic books of Old Testament
  - 224 Prophetic books of Old Testament

- 225 New Testament
- 226 Gospels & Acts
- 227 Epistles
- 228 Revelation (Apocalypse)
- 229 Apocrypha & pseudepigrapha

- 230 Christian theology
  - 231 God
  - 232 Jesus Christ & his family
  - 233 Humankind
  - 234 Salvation (Soteriology) & grace
  - 235 Spiritual beings
  - 236 Eschatology
  - *237 No longer used — formerly Future state*
  - 238 Creeds & catechisms
  - 239 Apologetics & polemics
- 240 Christian moral & devotional theology
  - 241 Moral theology
  - 242 Devotional literature
  - 243 Evangelistic writings for individuals
  - *244 No longer used — formerly Religious fiction*
  - *245 No longer used — formerly Hymnology*
  - 246 Use of art in Christianity
  - 247 Church furnishings & articles
  - 248 Christian experience, practice, life
  - 249 Christian observances in family life
- 250 Christian orders & local church
  - 251 Preaching (Homiletics)

- 252 Texts of sermons
- 253 Pastoral office (Pastoral theology)
- 254 Parish government & administration
- 255 Religious congregations & orders
- *256 No longer used — formerly Religious societies*
- *257 No longer used — formerly Parochial schools, libraries, etc.*
- *258 No longer used — formerly Parochial medicine*
- 259 Activities of the local church

- 260 Christian social theology
  - 261 Social theology
  - 262 Ecclesiology
  - 263 Times, places of religious observance
  - 264 Public worship
  - 265 Sacraments, other rites & acts
  - 266 Missions
  - 267 Associations for religious work
  - 268 Religious education
  - 269 Spiritual renewal
- 270 Christian church history
  - 271 Religious orders in church history
  - 272 Persecutions in church history
  - 273 Heresies in church history
  - 274 Christian church in Europe
  - 275 Christian church in Asia
  - 276 Christian church in Africa
  - 277 Christian church in North America

- 278 Christian church in South America
- 279 Christian church in other areas

- 280 Christian denominations & sects
  - 281 Early church & Eastern churches
  - 282 Roman Catholic Church
  - 283 Anglican churches
  - 284 Protestants of Continental origin
  - 285 Presbyterian, Reformed, Congregational
  - 286 Baptist, Disciples of Christ, Adventist
  - 287 Methodist & related churches
  - *288 No longer used — formerly Unitarian*
  - 289 Other denominations & sects
- 290 Other & comparative religions
  - 291 Comparative religion
  - 292 Classical (Greek & Roman) religion
  - 293 Germanic religion
  - 294 Religions of Indic origin
  - 295 Zoroastrianism (Mazdaism, Parseeism)
  - 296 Judaism
  - 297 Islam, Bábism & Bahá'í Faith
  - *298 No longer used — formerly Mormonism*
  - 299 Other religions

300 – Social Sciences

- 300 Social sciences
  - 301 Sociology & anthropology
  - 302 Social interaction
  - 303 Social processes

    - 304 Factors affecting social behavior
    - 305 Social groups
    - 306 Culture & institutions
    - 307 Communities
    - *308 No longer used — formerly Polygraphy*
    - *309 No longer used — formerly History of sociology*
- 310 General statistics
    - *311 No longer used — formerly Theory and methods*
    - *312 No longer used — formerly Population*
    - *313 No longer used — formerly Special topics*
    - 314 General statistics Of Europe
    - 315 General statistics Of Asia
    - 316 General statistics Of Africa
    - 317 General statistics Of North America
    - 318 General statistics Of South America
    - 319 General statistics Of other parts of the world
- 320 Political science
    - 321 Systems of governments & states
    - 322 Relation of state to organized groups
    - 323 Civil & political rights
    - 324 The political process
    - 325 International migration & colonization
    - 326 Slavery & emancipation
    - 327 International relations
    - 328 The legislative process
    - *329 Not assigned or no longer used*
- 330 Economics

- 331 Labor economics
- 332 Financial economics
- 333 Land economics
- 334 Cooperatives
- 335 Socialism & related systems
- 336 Public finance
- 337 International economics
- 338 Production
- 339 Macroeconomics & related topics

- 340 Law
  - 341 International law
  - 342 Constitutional & administrative law
  - 343 Military, tax, trade, industrial law
  - 344 Social, labor, welfare, & related law
  - 345 Criminal law
  - 346 Private law
  - 347 Civil procedure & courts
  - 348 Law (Statutes), regulations, cases
  - 349 Law of specific jurisdictions & areas
- 350 Public administration
  - 351 Of central governments
  - 352 Of local governments
  - 353 of U.S. federal & state governments
  - 354 Of specific central governments
  - 355 Military science
  - 356 Foot forces & warfare
  - 357 Mounted forces & warfare

- o 358 Other specialized forces & services
- o 359 Sea (Naval) forces & warfare

- 360 Social services; association
  - o 361 General social problems
  - o 362 Social welfare problems & services
  - o 363 Other social problems & services
  - o 364 Criminology
  - o 365 Penal & related institutions
  - o 366 Association
  - o 367 General clubs
  - o 368 Insurance
  - o 369 Miscellaneous kinds of associations
- 370 Education
  - o 371 School management; special education
  - o 372 Elementary education
  - o 373 Secondary education
  - o 374 Adult education
  - o 375 Curriculums
  - o *376 No longer used — formerly Education of women*
  - o *377 No longer used — formerly Ethical education*
  - o 378 Higher education
  - o 379 Government regulation, control, support
- 380 Commerce, communications, transport
  - o 381 Internal commerce (Domestic trade)
  - o 382 International commerce (Foreign trade)
  - o 383 Postal communication
  - o 384 Communications; Telecommunication

- o 385 Railroad transportation
- o 386 Inland waterway & ferry transportation
- o 387 Water, air, space transportation
- o 388 Transportation; Ground transportation
- o 389 Metrology & standardization

- 390 Customs, etiquette, folklore
  - o 391 Costume & personal appearance
  - o 392 Customs of life cycle & domestic life
  - o 393 Death customs
  - o 394 General customs
  - o 395 Etiquette (Manners)
  - o *396 No longer used — formerly Women's position and treatment*
  - o *397 No longer used — formerly outcast studies*
  - o 398 Folklore
  - o 399 Customs of war & diplomacy

400 – Language

- 400 Language
  - o 401 Philosophy & theory
  - o 402 Miscellany
  - o 403 Dictionaries & encyclopedias
  - o 404 Special topics
  - o 405 Serial publications
  - o 406 Organizations & management
  - o 407 Education, research, related topics
  - o 408 With respect to kinds of persons
  - o 409 Geographical & persons treatment

- 410 Linguistics
    - 411 Writing systems
    - 412 Etymology
    - 413 Dictionaries
    - 414 Phonology
    - 415 Structural systems (Grammar)
    - *416 No longer used — formerly Prosody*
    - 417 Dialectology & historical linguistics
    - 418 Standard usage; Applied linguistics
    - 419 Verbal language not spoken or written
- 420 English & Old English
    - 421 English writing system & phonology
    - 422 English etymology
    - 423 English dictionaries
    - *424 No longer used — formerly English thesauruses*
    - 425 English grammar
    - *426 No longer used — formerly English prosodies*
    - 427 English language variations
    - 428 Standard English usage
    - 429 Old English (Anglo-Saxon)
- 430 Germanic languages; German
    - 431 German writing system & phonology
    - 432 German etymology
    - 433 German dictionaries
    - *434 Not assigned or no longer used*
    - 435 German grammar
    - *436 Not assigned or no longer used*

- o 437 German language variations
- o 438 Standard German usage
- o 439 Other Germanic languages

- 440 Romance languages; French
  - o 441 French writing system & phonology
  - o 442 French etymology
  - o 443 French dictionaries
  - o *444 Not assigned or no longer used*
  - o 445 French grammar
  - o *446 Not assigned or no longer used*
  - o 447 French language variations
  - o 448 Standard French usage
  - o 449 Provencal & Catalan
- 450 Italian, Romanian, Rhaeto-Romanic
  - o 451 Italian writing system & phonology
  - o 452 Italian etymology
  - o 453 Italian dictionaries
  - o *454 Not assigned or no longer used*
  - o 455 Italian grammar
  - o *456 Not assigned or no longer used*
  - o 457 Italian language variations
  - o 458 Standard Italian usage
  - o 459 Romanian & Rhaeto-Romanic
- 460 Spanish & Portuguese languages
  - o 461 Spanish writing system & phonology
  - o 462 Spanish etymology
  - o 463 Spanish dictionaries

-
  - *464 Not assigned or no longer used*
  - 465 Spanish grammar
  - *466 Not assigned or no longer used*
  - 467 Spanish language variations
  - 468 Standard Spanish usage
  - 469 Portuguese
- 470 Italic; Latin
  - 471 Classical Latin writing & phonology
  - 472 Classical Latin etymology & phonology
  - 473 Classical Latin dictionaries
  - *474 Not assigned or no longer used*
  - 475 Classical Latin grammar
  - *476 Not assigned or no longer used*
  - 477 Old, Postclassical, Vulgar Latin
  - 478 Classical Latin usage
  - 479 Other Italic languages
- 480 Hellenic languages; Classical Greek
  - 481 Classical Greek writing & phonology
  - 482 Classical Greek etymology
  - 483 Classical Greek dictionaries
  - *484 Not assigned or no longer used*
  - 485 Classical Greek grammar
  - *486 Not assigned or no longer used*
  - 487 Preclassical & postclassical Greek
  - 488 Classical Greek usage
  - 489 Other Hellenic languages
- 490 Other languages

- 491 East Indo-European & Celtic languages
- 492 Afro-Asiatic languages; Semitic
- 493 Non-Semitic Afro-Asiatic languages
- 494 Ural-Altaic, Paleosiberian, Dravidian
- 495 Languages of East & Southeast Asia
- 496 African languages
- 497 North American native languages
- 498 South American native languages
- 499 Miscellaneous languages

500 – Science

- 500 Natural sciences & mathematics
  - 501 Philosophy & theory
  - 502 Miscellany
  - 503 Dictionaries & encyclopedias
  - *504 Not assigned or no longer used*
  - 505 Serial publications
  - 506 Organizations & management
  - 507 Education, research, related topics
  - 508 Natural history
  - 509 Historical, areas, persons treatment
- 510 Mathematics
  - 511 General principles
  - 512 Algebra & number theory
  - 513 Arithmetic
  - 514 Topology
  - 515 Analysis
  - 516 Geometry

  - *517 Not assigned or no longer used*
  - 518 Numerical analysis
  - 519 Probabilities & applied mathematics
- 520 Astronomy & allied sciences
  - 521 Celestial mechanics
  - 522 Techniques, equipment, materials
  - 523 Specific celestial bodies & phenomena
  - *524 Not assigned or no longer used*
  - 525 Earth (Astronomical geography)
  - 526 Mathematical geography
  - 527 Celestial navigation
  - 528 Ephemerides
  - 529 Chronology
- 530 Physics
  - 531 Classical mechanics; Solid mechanics
  - 532 Fluid mechanics; Liquid mechanics
  - 533 Gas mechanics
  - 534 Sound & related vibrations
  - 535 Light & paraphotic phenomena
  - 536 Heat
  - 537 Electricity & electronics
  - 538 Magnetism
  - 539 Modern physics
- 540 Chemistry & allied sciences
  - 541 Physical & theoretical chemistry
  - 542 Techniques, equipment, materials
  - 543 Analytical chemistry

- 544 Qualitative analysis
- 545 Quantitative analysis
- 546 Inorganic chemistry
- 547 Organic chemistry
- 548 Crystallography
- 549 Mineralogy

- 550 Earth sciences
  - 551 Geology, hydrology, meteorology
  - 552 Petrology
  - 553 Economic geology
  - 554 Earth sciences of Europe
  - 555 Earth sciences of Asia
  - 556 Earth sciences of Africa
  - 557 Earth sciences of North America
  - 558 Earth sciences of South America
  - 559 Earth sciences of other areas
- 560 Paleontology; Paleozoology
  - 561 Paleobotany
  - 562 Fossil invertebrates
  - 563 Fossil primitive phyla
  - 564 Fossil Mollusca & Molluscoidea
  - 565 Other fossil invertebrates
  - 566 Fossil Vertebrata (Fossil Craniata)
  - 567 Fossil cold-blooded vertebrates
  - 568 Fossil Aves (Fossil birds)
  - 569 Fossil Mammalia
- 570 Life sciences

  - o 571 Physiology
  - o 572 Biochemistry
  - o 573 Physiological systems of animals
  - o *574 Not assigned or no longer used*
  - o 575 Physiological systems of plants
  - o 576 Genetics and evolution
  - o 577 Ecology
  - o 578 Natural history of organisms
  - o 579 Microorganisms, fungi, algae
- 580 Plants
  - o 581 Botany
  - o 582 Plants noted for specific vegetative characteristics and flowers
  - o 583 Dicotyledones
  - o 584 Monocotyledones
  - o 585 Gymnospermae (Pinophyta)
  - o 586 Cryptogamia (Seedless plants)
  - o 587 Pteridophyta (Vascular cryptogams)
  - o 588 Bryophyta
  - o *589 Not assigned or no longer used*
- 590 Zoological sciences
  - o 591 Zoology
  - o 592 Invertebrates
  - o 593 Protozoa, Echinodermata, related phyla
  - o 594 Mollusca & Molluscoidea
  - o 595 Other invertebrates
  - o 596 Vertebrata (Craniata, Vertebrates)

- o 597 Cold-blooded vertebrates, fishes
- o 598 Aves (Birds)
- o 599 Mammalia (Mammals)

600 – Technology

- 600 Technology (Applied sciences)
  - o 601 Philosophy & theory
  - o 602 Miscellany
  - o 603 Dictionaries & encyclopedias
  - o 604 Special topics
  - o 605 Serial publications
  - o 606 Organizations
  - o 607 Education, research, related topics
  - o 608 Invention & patents
  - o 609 Historical, areas, persons treatment
- 610 Medical sciences; Medicine
  - o 611 Human anatomy, cytology, histology
  - o 612 Human physiology
  - o 613 Promotion of health
  - o 614 Incidence & prevention of disease
  - o 615 Pharmacology & therapeutics
  - o 616 Diseases
  - o 617 Surgery & related medical specialties
  - o 618 Gynecology & other medical specialties
  - o 619 Experimental medicine
- 620 Engineering & Applied operations
  - o 621 Applied physics
  - o 622 Mining & related operations

    - 623 Military & nautical engineering
    - 624 Civil engineering
    - 625 Engineering of railroads, roads
    - *626 Not assigned or no longer used*
    - 627 Hydraulic engineering
    - 628 Sanitary & municipal engineering
    - 629 Other branches of engineering
- 630 Agriculture
    - 631 Techniques, equipment, materials
    - 632 Plant injuries, diseases, pests
    - 633 Field & plantation crops
    - 634 Orchards, fruits, forestry
    - 635 Garden crops (Horticulture)
    - 636 Animal husbandry
    - 637 Processing dairy & related products
    - 638 Insect culture
    - 639 Hunting, fishing, conservation
- 640 Home economics & family living
    - 641 Food & drink
    - 642 Meals & table service
    - 643 Housing & household equipment
    - 644 Household utilities
    - 645 Household furnishings
    - 646 Sewing, clothing, personal living
    - 647 Management of public households
    - 648 Housekeeping
    - 649 Child rearing & home care of sick

- 650 Management & auxiliary services
  - o 651 Office services
  - o 652 Processes of written communication
  - o 653 Shorthand
  - o *654 Not assigned or no longer used*
  - o *655 Not assigned or no longer used*
  - o *656 Not assigned or no longer used*
  - o 657 Accounting
  - o 658 General management
  - o 659 Advertising & public relations
- 660 Chemical engineering
  - o 661 Industrial chemicals technology
  - o 662 Explosives, fuels technology
  - o 663 Beverage technology
  - o 664 Food technology
  - o 665 Industrial oils, fats, waxes, gases
  - o 666 Ceramic & allied technologies
  - o 667 Cleaning, color, related technologies
  - o 668 Technology of other organic products
  - o 669 Metallurgy
- 670 Manufacturing
  - o 671 Metalworking & metal products
  - o 672 Iron, steel, other iron alloys
  - o 673 Nonferrous metals
  - o 674 Lumber processing, wood products, cork
  - o 675 Leather & fur processing
  - o 676 Pulp & paper technology

- o 677 Textiles
- o 678 Elastomers & elastomer products
- o 679 Other products of specific materials

- 680 Manufacture for specific uses
  - o 681 Precision instruments & other devices
  - o 682 Small forge work (Blacksmithing)
  - o 683 Hardware & household appliances
  - o 684 Furnishings & home workshops
  - o 685 Leather, fur, related products
  - o 686 Printing & related activities
  - o 687 Clothing
  - o 688 Other final products & packaging
  - o *689 Not assigned or no longer used*
- 690 Buildings
  - o 691 Building materials
  - o 692 Auxiliary construction practices
  - o 693 Specific materials & purposes
  - o 694 Wood construction; Carpentry
  - o 695 Roof covering
  - o 696 Utilities
  - o 697 Heating, ventilating, air-conditioning
  - o 698 Detail finishing
  - o *699 Not assigned or no longer used*

700 – Arts and Recreation

- 700 The arts
  - o 701 Philosophy & theory
  - o 702 Miscellany

- 703 Dictionaries & encyclopedias
- 704 Special topics
- 705 Serial publications
- 706 Organizations & management
- 707 Education, research, related topics
- 708 Galleries, museums, private collections
- 709 Historical, areas, persons treatment

- 710 Civic & landscape art
  - 711 Area planning (Civic art)
  - 712 Landscape architecture
  - 713 Landscape architecture of trafficways
  - 714 Water features
  - 715 Woody plants
  - 716 Herbaceous plants
  - 717 Structures
  - 718 Landscape design of cemeteries
  - 719 Natural landscapes
- 720 Architecture
  - 721 Architectural structure
  - 722 Architecture to ca. 300
  - 723 Architecture from ca. 300 to 1399
  - 724 Architecture from 1400
  - 725 Public structures
  - 726 Buildings for religious purposes
  - 727 Buildings for education & research
  - 728 Residential & related buildings
  - 729 Design & decoration

- 730 Plastic arts; Sculpture
  - o 731 Processes, forms, subjects of sculpture
  - o 732 Sculpture to ca. 500
  - o 733 Greek, Etruscan, Roman sculpture
  - o 734 Sculpture from ca. 500 to 1399
  - o 735 Sculpture from 1400
  - o 736 Carving & carvings
  - o 737 Numismatics & sigillography
  - o 738 Ceramic arts
  - o 739 Art metalwork
- 740 Drawing & decorative arts
  - o 741 Drawing & drawings
  - o 742 Perspective (graphical)
  - o 743 Drawing & drawings by subject
  - o *744 Not assigned or no longer used*
  - o 745 Decorative arts
  - o 746 Textile arts
  - o 747 Interior decoration
  - o 748 Glass
  - o 749 Furniture & accessories
- 750 Painting & paintings
  - o 751 Techniques, equipment, forms
  - o 752 Color
  - o 753 Symbolism, allegory, mythology, legend
  - o 754 Genre paintings
  - o 755 Religion & religious symbolism
  - o *756 Not assigned or no longer used*

  - 757 Human figures & their parts
  - 758 Other subjects
  - 759 Historical, areas, persons treatment
- 760 Graphic arts; Printmaking & prints
  - 761 Relief processes (Block printing)
  - *762 Not assigned or no longer used*
  - 763 Lithographic (Planographic) processes
  - 764 Chromolithography & serigraphy
  - 765 Metal engraving
  - 766 Mezzotinting & related processes
  - 767 Etching & drypoint
  - *768 Not assigned or no longer used*
  - 769 Prints
- 770 Photography & photographs
  - 771 Techniques, equipment, materials
  - 772 Metallic salt processes
  - 773 Pigment processes of printing
  - 774 Holography
  - 775 Digital photography
  - 776 Computer art
  - *777 Not assigned or no longer used*
  - 778 Fields & kinds of photography
  - 779 Photographs
- 780 Music
  - 781 General principles & musical forms
  - 782 Vocal music
  - 783 Music for single voices; The voice

  - 784 Instruments & Instrumental ensembles
  - 785 Chamber music
  - 786 Keyboard & other instruments
  - 787 Stringed instruments (Chordophones)
  - 788 Wind instruments (Aerophones)
  - *789 Not assigned or no longer used*
- 790 Recreational & performing arts
  - 791 Public performances
  - 792 Stage presentations
  - 793 Indoor games & amusements
  - 794 Indoor games of skill
  - 795 Games of chance
  - 796 Athletic & outdoor sports & games
  - 797 Aquatic & air sports
  - 798 Equestrian sports & animal racing
  - 799 Fishing, hunting, shooting

800 – Literature

- 800 Literature & rhetoric
  - 801 Philosophy & theory
  - 802 Miscellany
  - 803 Dictionaries & encyclopedias
  - *804 Not assigned or no longer used*
  - 805 Serial publications
  - 806 Organizations
  - 807 Education, research, related topics
  - 808 Rhetoric & collections of literature
  - 809 Literary history & criticism

- 810 American literature in English
  - 811 Poetry
  - 812 Drama
  - 813 Fiction
  - 814 Essays
  - 815 Speeches
  - 816 Letters
  - 817 Satire & humor
  - 818 Miscellaneous writings
  - *819 Not assigned or no longer used*
- 820 English & Old English literatures
  - 821 English poetry
  - 822 English drama
  - 823 English fiction
  - 824 English essays
  - 825 English speeches
  - 826 English letters
  - 827 English satire & humor
  - 828 English miscellaneous writings
  - 829 Old English (Anglo-Saxon)
- 830 Literatures of Germanic languages
  - 831 German poetry
  - 832 German drama
  - 833 German fiction
  - 834 German essays
  - 835 German speeches
  - 836 German letters

  - 837 German satire & humor
  - 838 German miscellaneous writings
  - 839 Other Germanic literatures
- 840 Literatures of Romance languages
  - 841 French poetry
  - 842 French drama
  - 843 French fiction
  - 844 French essays
  - 845 French speeches
  - 846 French letters
  - 847 French satire & humor
  - 848 French miscellaneous writings
  - 849 Provencal & Catalan
- 850 Italian, Romanian, Rhaeto-Romanic
  - 851 Italian poetry
  - 852 Italian drama
  - 853 Italian fiction
  - 854 Italian essays
  - 855 Italian speeches
  - 856 Italian letters
  - 857 Italian satire & humor
  - 858 Italian miscellaneous writings
  - 859 Romanian & Rhaeto-Romanic
- 860 Spanish & Portuguese literatures
  - 861 Spanish poetry
  - 862 Spanish drama
  - 863 Spanish fiction

- o 864 Spanish essays
- o 865 Spanish speeches
- o 866 Spanish letters
- o 867 Spanish satire & humor
- o 868 Spanish miscellaneous writings
- o 869 Portuguese

- 870 Italic literatures; Latin
    - o 871 Latin poetry
    - o 872 Latin dramatic poetry & drama
    - o 873 Latin epic poetry & fiction
    - o 874 Latin lyric poetry
    - o 875 Latin speeches
    - o 876 Latin letters
    - o 877 Latin satire & humor
    - o 878 Latin miscellaneous writings
    - o 879 Literatures of other Italic languages
- 880 Hellenic literatures; Classical Greek
    - o 881 Classical Greek poetry
    - o 882 Classical Greek drama
    - o 883 Classical Greek epic poetry & fiction
    - o 884 Classical Greek lyric poetry
    - o 885 Classical Greek speeches
    - o 886 Classical Greek letters
    - o 887 Classical Greek satire & humor
    - o 888 Classical Greek miscellaneous writings
    - o 889 Modern Greek
- 890 Literatures of other languages

    - 891 East Indo-European & Celtic
    - 892 Afro-Asiatic literatures Semitic
    - 893 Non-Semitic Afro-Asiatic literatures
    - 894 Ural-Altaic, Paleosiberian, Dravidian
    - 895 Literatures of East & Southeast Asia
    - 896 African literatures
    - 897 North American native literatures
    - 898 South American native literatures
    - 899 Other literatures

900 – History, Geography, and Biography

- 900 Geography & history
    - 901 Philosophy & theory
    - 902 Miscellany
    - 903 Dictionaries & encyclopedias
    - 904 Collected accounts of events
    - 905 Serial publications
    - 906 Organizations & management
    - 907 Education, research, related topics
    - 908 With respect to kinds of persons
    - 909 World history
- 910 Geography & travel
    - 911 Historical geography
    - 912 Graphic representations of earth
    - 913 Ancient world
    - 914 Europe
    - 915 Asia
    - 916 Africa

- o 917 North America
- o 918 South America
- o 919 Other areas
- • 920 Biography, genealogy, insignia
  - o *921 Not assigned or no longer used*
  - o *922 Not assigned or no longer used*
  - o *923 Not assigned or no longer used*
  - o *924 Not assigned or no longer used*
  - o *925 Not assigned or no longer used*
  - o *926 Not assigned or no longer used*
  - o *927 Not assigned or no longer used*
  - o *928 Not assigned or no longer used*
    - – The 921-928 range is reserved as an optional location for biographies, which are shelved alphabetically by subject's last name.
  - o 929 Genealogy, names, insignia
- • 930 History of ancient world
  - o 931 History of ancient world; China
  - o 932 History of ancient world; Egypt
  - o 933 History of ancient world; Palestine
  - o 934 History of ancient world; India
  - o 935 History of ancient world; Mesopotamia & Iranian Plateau
  - o 936 History of ancient world; Europe north & west of Italy
  - o 937 History of ancient world; Italy & adjacent territories
  - o 938 History of ancient world; Greece

    - o 939 History of ancient world; Other parts of ancient world
- 940 General history of Europe
    - o 941 General history of Europe; British Isles
    - o 942 General history of Europe; England & Wales
    - o 943 General history of Europe; Central Europe Germany
    - o 944 General history of Europe; France & Monaco
    - o 945 General history of Europe; Italian Peninsula & adjacent islands
    - o 946 General history of Europe; Iberian Peninsula & adjacent islands
    - o 947 General history of Europe; Eastern Europe; Soviet Union
    - o 948 General history of Europe; Northern Europe; Scandinavia
    - o 949 General history of Europe; Other parts of Europe
- 950 General history of Asia; Far East
    - o 951 General history of Asia; China & adjacent areas
    - o 952 General history of Asia; Japan
    - o 953 General history of Asia; Arabian Peninsula & adjacent areas
    - o 954 General history of Asia; South Asia; India
    - o 955 General history of Asia; Iran
    - o 956 General history of Asia; Middle East (Near East)
    - o 957 General history of Asia; Siberia (Asiatic Russia)

- 958 General history of Asia; Central Asia
- 959 General history of Asia; Southeast Asia

- 960 General history of Africa
  - 961 General history of Africa; Tunisia & Libya
  - 962 General history of Africa; Egypt & Sudan
  - 963 General history of Africa; Ethiopia
  - 964 General history of Africa; Morocco & Canary Islands
  - 965 General history of Africa; Algeria
  - 966 General history of Africa; West Africa & offshore islands
  - 967 General history of Africa; Central Africa & offshore islands
  - 968 General history of Africa; Southern Africa
  - 969 General history of Africa; South Indian Ocean islands
- 970 General history of North America
  - 971 General history of North America; Canada
  - 972 General history of North America; Middle America; Mexico
  - 973 General history of North America; United States
  - 974 General history of North America; Northeastern United States
  - 975 General history of North America; Southeastern United States
  - 976 General history of North America; South central United States
  - 977 General history of North America; North central United States

  - o 978 General history of North America; Western United States
  - o 979 General history of North America; Great Basin & Pacific Slope
- 980 General history of South America
  - o 981 General history of South America; Brazil
  - o 982 General history of South America; Argentina
  - o 983 General history of South America; Chile
  - o 984 General history of South America; Bolivia
  - o 985 General history of South America; Peru
  - o 986 General history of South America; Colombia & Ecuador
  - o 987 General history of South America; Venezuela
  - o 988 General history of South America; Guiana
  - o 989 General history of South America; Paraguay & Uruguay
- 990 General history of other areas
  - o *991 Not assigned or no longer used*
  - o *992 Not assigned or no longer used*
  - o 993 General history of other areas; New Zealand
  - o 994 General history of other areas; Australia
  - o 995 General history of other areas; Melanesia; New Guinea
  - o 996 General history of other areas; Other parts of Pacific Polynesia
  - o 997 General history of other areas; Atlantic Ocean islands
  - o 998 General history of other areas; Arctic islands & Antarctica
  - o 999 Extraterrestrial worlds

BLISS BIBLIOGRAPHIC CLASSIFICATION

Remarkable, the Bliss bibliographic classification (BC) is a library classification system that was created by Henry E. Bliss (1870–1955), published in four volumes between 1940 and 1953. Although originally devised in the United States, it was more commonly adopted by British libraries than by American ones. A second edition of the system (BC2) has been developed in Britain since 1977.

Bliss was born in New York in 1870 and in 1891 began work in the library of the College of the City of New York (now City College of the City University of New York). Bliss had a lifelong interest in the organization, structure and philosophy of knowledge and was very critical of the library classification systems that were available to him. He believed that because the popular Library of Congress system had been designed for a specific library (the Library of Congress) it had no use as a standard system outside that library. He also greatly disliked the Dewey Decimal system.

Bliss wanted a classification system that would provide distinct rules yet still be adaptable to whatever kind of collection a library might have, as different libraries have different needs. His solution was the concept of "alternative location," in which a particular subject could be put in more than one place, as long as the library made a specific choice and used it consistently. In 1908 Bliss reclassified 60,000 of his library's books, and in 1910 he published an article with a rough scheme of his general ideas. But as he continued to develop his system he realized that it was going to be a much larger project than he had anticipated. The first of his four volumes appeared in 1940 (the year he retired) and the last in 1953, two years before his death.

It is remarkable, that of the underlying policies of the BC system were:

(a) alternative location

(b) brief, concise notation

(c) organizing knowledge according to academic expertise

(d) subjects moving gradually from topic to topic as they naturally related to one another.

Illustration

Bliss deliberately avoided the use of the decimal point because of his objection to Dewey's system. Instead he used capital and lower-case letters, numerals, and every typographical symbol available on his extensive and somewhat eccentric typewriter.

In the revised edition (BC2), only capital letters are used, with numerals occasionally used for special purposes. Here is an extract:

HJ	Preventive medicine
. . .	
HL	Curative medicine
HLK	Primary care; general practice
HLY	Secondary care, aftercare

BC was not used by many North American libraries. The system was not without its flaws (the result of being largely a one-person project), and the layout of Bliss's text was difficult to read. A few library schools sometimes taught the BC system to their students, but only in a minor way. The failure of the system to catch on in North America was partly because of its internal deficiencies but also because the Dewey Decimal and Library of Congress systems were already well established. The City College library continued to use Bliss's system until 1967, when it reluctantly switched to the Library of Congress system. It had become too expensive to train new staff members to use BC, and too expensive to maintain in general. Much of the Bliss stacks remain, however, as no-one has recatalogued the books. The case was different, however, in Britain. BC proved more popular there and also spread to other English-speaking countries. Part of the reason for its success was that libraries in teachers' colleges liked the way Bliss had organized the subject areas on teaching and education. By the mid-1950s the system was being used in at least sixty British libraries and in a hundred by the 1970s.

It is remarkable that 1967 the Bliss Classification Association was formed. Its first publication was the *Abridged Bliss Classification* (ABC), intended for school libraries. In 1977 it began to publish and maintain a much-improved, revised version of Bliss's system, the Bliss Bibliographic Classification (Second Edition) or BC2. This retains only the broad outlines of Bliss's scheme, replacing most of the detailed notation with a new scheme based on the principles of faceted classification. Fifteen of approximately 28 volumes of schedules have so far been published.

BCM CLASSIFICATION

Basically, British Catalogue of Music Classification (BCM Classification) is a faceted classification that was commissioned from E. J. Coates by the Council of the British National Bibliography to organize the content of the British Catalogue of Music. The published schedule (1960) was considerably expanded by Patrick Mills of the British Library up until its use was abandoned in 1998. Entries in the catalogue were organized by BCM classmark from the catalogue's inception in 1957 until 1982. From that year the British Catalogue of Music (which from 1974 onward was published by The British Library) was organized instead by Dewey Decimal Classification number, though BCM classmarks continued to be added to entries up to the 1998 annual cumulation. The schedule is divided into two main parts: A-B representing Musical literature and C-Z representing Music — Scores and Parts. There are also seven auxiliary tables dealing with various sub-arrangements, sets of ethnic/locality subdivisions and chronological reference points.

The notation is retroactive using uppercase alphabetic characters omitting I and O, with the addition of slash / and parentheses ( ) which have specific anteriorizing functions. Retroactive notation requires that the classifier combines terms in reverse schedule order. This has the benefit of producing a compact notation by removing the need for facet indicators.

The schedule at A (Music Literature) parallels that from the Scores and Parts schedules thus Choral Music is at D while books about Choral Music are at AD; Harp Music is at TQ so books on harp music are at ATQ. The schedule at B accommodates books about specific composers and music in non-European traditions.

As a fully faceted scheme after the ideas of S. R. Ranganathan, BCM class numbers are capable of being chain-indexed, allowing index access to each step of the hierarchy.

BCM classification had a strong influence on Russell Sweeney's so-called Phoenix Dewey 780 schedule which in turn influenced the 780 Music schedule in the 20th edition of Dewey Decimal Classification. The music schedule of the second edition of the Bliss Classification is also strongly influenced by BCM.

NATIONAL LIBRARY OF MEDICINE CLASSIFICATION

The National Library of Medicine (NLM) classification system is a library indexing system covering the fields of medicine and preclinical basic sciences. The NLM classification is patterned after the Library of Congress (LC) Classification system: alphabetical letters denote broad subject categories which are subdivided by numbers. For example, *QW 279* would indicate a book on an aspect of microbiology or immunology. The one- or two-letter alphabetical codes in the NLM classification use a limited range of letters: only QS–QZ and W–WZ. This allows the NLM system to co-exist with the larger LC coding scheme as neither of these ranges are used in the LC system. There are, however, three pre-existing codes in the LC system which overlap with the NLM: *Human Anatomy* (QM), *Microbiology* (QR), and *Medicine* (R). To avoid further confusion, these three codes are not used in the NLM.

Notably, the headings for the individual *schedules* (letters or letter pairs) are given in brief form (e.g., QW - *Microbiology and Immunology*; WG - *Cardiovascular System*) and together they provide an outline of the subjects covered by the NLM classification. Headings are interpreted broadly and include the physiological system, the specialties connected with them, the regions of the body chiefly concerned and subordinate related fields. The NLM system is hierarchical, and within each schedule, division by organ usually has priority. Each main schedule, as well as some sub-sections, begins with a group of form numbers ranging generally from 1–49 which classify materials by publication type, e.g., dictionaries, atlases, laboratory manuals, etc. The main schedules QS-QZ, W-WY, and WZ (excluding the range WZ 220–270) classify works published after 1913; the 19th century schedule is used for works published 1801-1913; and WZ 220-270 is used to provide century groupings for works published before 1801.

Main Categories

Preclinical Sciences

- QS Human Anatomy
- QT Physiology

- QU Biochemistry
- QV Pharmacology
- QW Microbiology & Immunology
- QX Parasitology
- QY Clinical Pathology
- QZ Pathology

Medicine and Related Subjects

- W Health Professions
- WA Public Health
- WB Practice of Medicine
- WC Communicable Diseases
- WD Disorders of Systemic, Metabolic, or Environmental Origin, etc.
- WE Musculoskeletal System
- WF Respiratory System
- WG Cardiovascular System
- WH Hemic and Lymphatic Systems
- WI Digestive System
- WJ Urogenital System
- WK Endocrine System
- WL Nervous System
- WM Psychiatry
- WN Radiology. Diagnostic Imaging
- WO Surgery
- WP Gynecology
- WQ Obstetrics
- WR Dermatology

- WS Pediatrics
- WT Geriatrics. Chronic Disease
- WU Dentistry. Oral Surgery
- WV Otolaryngology
- WW Ophthalmology
- WX Hospitals & Other Health Facilities
- WY Nursing
- WZ History of Medicine
- 19th Century Schedule

DICKINSON CLASSIFICATION

The Dickinson classification is a library classification scheme used to catalogue and classify musical compositions. It is fully detailed by Carol June Bradley in *The Dickinson classification : a cataloguing & classification manual for music;* including a reprint of the *George Sherman Dickinson Classification of Musical Compositions* published by Carlisle Books (1968).

NEW CLASSIFICATION SCHEME FOR CHINESE LIBRARIES

The New Classification Scheme for Chinese Libraries is a system of library classification developed by Yung-Hsiang Lai since 1956. It is modified from "A System of Book Classification for Chinese Libraries" of Liu Guojun, which is based on the Dewey Decimal System.

The scheme is developed for Chinese books, and commonly used in Taiwan, Hong Kong and Macau.

Main Classes

- 000 Generalities
- 100 Philosophy

- 200 Religion
- 300 Sciences
- 400 Applied sciences
- 500 Social sciences
- 600-700 History and Geography
- 800 Linguistics and Literature
- 900 Arts

Outline of the Classification Tables

- 000 Generalities
  - o 000 Special collections
  - o 010 Bibliography; Literacy (Documentation)
  - o 020 Library and information science; Archive management
  - o 030 Sinology
  - o 040 General encyclopedia
  - o 050 Serial publications; Periodicals
  - o 060 General organization; Museology
  - o 070 General collected essays
  - o 080 General series
  - o 090 Collected Chinese classics
- 100 Philosophy
  - o 100 Philosoply: general
  - o 110 Thought; Learning
  - o 120 Chinese philosophy
  - o 130 Oriental philosophy
  - o 140 Western philosophy
  - o 150 Logic

    - 160 Metaphysics
    - 170 Psychology
    - 180 Esthetics
    - 190 Ethics
- 200 Religion
    - 200 Religion: general
    - 210 Science of religion
    - 220 Buddhism
    - 230 Taoism
    - 240 Christianity
    - 250 Islam (Mohammedanism)
    - 260 Judaism
    - 270 Other religions
    - 280 Mythology
    - 290 Astrology; Superstition
- 300 Sciences
    - 300 Sciences: general
    - 310 Mathematics
    - 320 Astronomy
    - 330 Physics
    - 340 Chemistry
    - 350 Earth science; Geology
    - 360 Biological science
    - 370 Botany
    - 380 Zoology
    - 390 Anthropology
- 400 Applied sciences

  - 400 Applied sciences: general
  - 410 Medical sciences
  - 420 Home economics
  - 430 Agriculture
  - 440 Engineering
  - 450 Mining and metallurgy
  - 460 Chemical engineering
  - 470 Manufacture
  - 480 Commerce: various business
  - 490 Commerce: administration and management
- 500 Social sciences
  - 500 Social sciences: general
  - 510 Statistics
  - 520 Education
  - 530 Rite and custom
  - 540 Sociology
  - 550 Economy
  - 560 Finance
  - 570 Political science
  - 580 Law; Jurisprudence
  - 590 Military science
- 600-700 History and geography
  - 600 History and geography: General
- History and geography of China
  - 610 General history of China
  - 620 Chinese history by period
  - 630 History of Chinese civilization

   - 640 Diplomatic history of China
   - 650 Historical sources
   - 660 Geography of China
   - 670 Local history
   - 680 Topicla topography
   - 690 Chinese travels
- World history and geography
   - 710 World: general history and geography
   - 720 Oceans and seas
   - 730 Asia: history and geography
   - 740 Europe: history and geography
   - 750 America: history and geography
   - 760 Africa: history and geography
   - 770 Oceania: history and geography
   - 780 Biography
   - 790 Antiquities & archaeology
- 800 Linguistics and literature
   - 800 Linguistics: general
   - 810 Literature: general
   - 820 Chinese literature
   - 830 Chinese literature: general collections
   - 840 Chinese literature: indivisual works
   - 850 Various Chinese literature
   - 860 Oriental literature
   - 870 Western literature
   - 880 Other countries literatures
   - 890 Journalism

- 900 Arts
  - 900 Arts: general
  - 910 Music
  - 920 Architecture
  - 930 Sculpture
  - 940 Drawing & painting; Calligraphy
  - 950 Photography ; Computer art
  - 960 Decorative arts
  - 970 Arts and crafts
  - 980 Theatre
  - 990 Recreation and leisure

CITATION

In common parlance, a citation is a reference to a published or unpublished source (not always the original source). More precisely, a citation is an abbreviated alphanumeric expression (e.g. [Newell84]) embedded in the body of an intellectual work that denotes an entry in the bibliographic references section of the work for the purpose of acknowledging the relevance of the works of others to the topic of discussion at the spot where the citation appears. Generally the combination of both the in-body citation and the bibliographic entry constitutes what is commonly thought of as a citation (whereas bibliographic entries by themselves are not). A prime purpose of a citation is intellectual honesty; to attribute to other authors the ideas they have previously expressed, rather than give the appearance to the work's readers that the work's authors are the original wellsprings of those ideas.

Notably, forms of citations generally subscribe to one of the generally-accepted citations systems, such as the Harvard,

APA, and other citations systems, as their syntactic conventions are widely-known and easily interpreted by readers. Each of these citation systems has its respective advantages and disadvantages relative to the tradeoffs of being informative (but not too disruptive) and thus should be chosen relative to the needs of the type of publication being crafted. Editors will often specify the citation system to use. Bibliographies, and other list-like compilations of references, are generally not considered citations because they do not fulfill the true spirit of the term: deliberate acknowledgement by other authors of the priority of one's ideas.

A bibliographic citation is a reference to a book, article, web page, or other published item. Citations should supply sufficient detail to identify the item uniquely. Different citation systems and styles are used in scientific citation, legal citation, prior art, and the arts and the humanities. A citation number, used in some citation systems, is a number or symbol added inline and usually in superscript, to refer readers to a footnote or endnote that cites the source. In other citation systems, an inline parenthetical reference is used rather than a citation number, with limited information such as the author's last name, year of publication, and page number referenced; a full identification of the source will then appear in an appended bibliography.

Citation Content

Citation content can vary depending on the type of source and may include:

1. *Journal:* article title, journal title, date of publication, and page number(s).
2. *Book:* author(s), book title, publisher, date of publication, and page number(s) if appropriate.
3. *Newspaper:* author(s), article title, name of newspaper,

section title and page number(s) if desired, date of publication.

4. *Web site:* author(s), article and publication title where appropriate, as well as a URL, and a date when the site was accessed.
5. *Poem:* spaced slashes are normally used to indicate separate lines of a poem, and parenthetical citations usually include the line number(s). For example: "For I must love because I live / And life in me is what you give." (Brennan, lines 15–16).
6. *Play:* inline citations offer part, scene, and line numbers, the latter separated by periods: 4.452 refers to scene 4, line 452. For example, "In Eugene Onegin, Onegin rejects Tanya when she is free to be his, and only decides he wants her when she is already married" (Pushkin 4.452-53).

Unique Identifiers

Along with information such as author(s), date of publication, title and page numbers, citations may also include unique identifiers depending on the type of work being referred to.

(a) Citations of books may include an International Standard Book Number (ISBN).

(b) Specific volumes, articles or other identifiable parts of a periodical, may have an associated Serial Item and Contribution Identifier (SICI).

(c) Electronic documents may have a digital object identifier (DOI).

(d) Biomedical research articles may have a PubMed Identifier (PMID).

Note Systems

Note systems involve the use of sequential numbers in the text which refer to either footnotes (notes at the end of the page) or endnotes (a note on a separate page at the end of the paper) which gives the source detail. The notes system may or may not require a full bibliography, depending on whether the writer has used a full note form or a shortened note form.

For example, an excerpt from the text of a paper using a notes system *without a full bibliography* could look like this:

> "The five stages of grief are denial, anger, bargaining, depression, and acceptance."1

The note, located either at the foot of the page (footnote) or at the end of the paper (endnote) would look like this:

1. Elisabeth Kübler-Ross, *On Death and Dying* (New York: Macmillan, 1969) 45–60.

In a paper which contains a full bibliography, the shortened note could look like this:

1. Kübler-Ross, *On Death and Dying* 45–60.

and the bibliography entry, which would be required with a shortened note, would look like this:

Kübler-Ross, Elisabeth. *On Death and Dying*. New York: Macmillan, 1969.

Citation Styles

- *ACS Style Guide*
- *The Associated Press Stylebook*
- *The Chicago Manual of Style*
- *Turabian*

- *The Elements of Style*
- *The Elements of Typographic Style*
- *ISO 690*
- *MHRA Style Guide*
- *MLA Handbook*
- *MLA Style Manual*
- *The New York Times Manual*
- *The Oxford Guide to Style/New Hart's Rules*
- *The Publication Manual of the APA*

Citation styles can be broadly divided into styles common to the Humanities and the Sciences, though there is considerable overlap. Some style guides, such as the Chicago Manual of Style, are quite flexible and cover both parenthetical and note citation systems. Others, such as MLA and APA styles, specify formats within the context of a single citation system. These may be referred to as citation formats as well as citation styles. The various guides thus specify order of appearance, for example, of publication date, title, and page numbers following the author name, in addition to conventions of punctuation, use of italics, emphasis, parenthesis, quotation marks, etc., particular to their style.

A number of organizations have created styles to fit their needs; consequently, a number of different guides exist. Individual publishers often have their own in-house variations as well, and some works are so long-established as to have their own citation methods too: Stephanus pagination for Plato; Bekker numbers for Aristotle; citing the Bible by book, chapter and verse; or Shakespeare notation by play, act and scene.

Humanities

- The American Political Science Association (APSA) relies on the *Style Manual for Political Science,* a style often used by political science scholars and historians. It is largely based on that of the Chicago Manual of Style.
- The ASA style of American Sociological Association is one of the main styles used in sociological publications.
- The Chicago Style (CMOS) was developed and its guide is *The Chicago Manual of Style.* Some social sciences and humanities scholars use the nearly identical Turabian style. Used by writers in many fields.
- The Columbia Style was made by Janice R. Walker and Todd Taylor to give detailed guidelines for citing internet sources. Columbia Style offers models for both the humanities and the sciences.
- *Evidence Explained: Citing History Sources from Artifacts to Cyberspace* by Elizabeth Shown Mills covers primary sources not included in CMOS, such as censuses, court, land, government, business, and church records. Includes sources in electronic format. Used by genealogists and historians.
- Harvard referencing (or author-date system) is a specific kind of parenthetical referencing. Parenthetical referencing is recommended by both the British Standards Institution and the Modern Language Association. Harvard referencing involves a short author-date reference, e.g., "(Smith, 2000)", being inserted after the cited text within parentheses and the full reference to the source being listed at the end of the article.

- MLA style was developed by the Modern Language Association and is most often used in the arts and the humanities, particularly in English studies, other literary studies, including comparative literature and literary criticism in languages other than English ("foreign languages"), and some interdisciplinary studies, such as cultural studies, drama and theatre, film, and other media, including television. This style of citations and bibliographical format uses parenthetical referencing with author-page (Smith 395) or author-[short] title-page (Smith, *Contingencies* 42) in the case of more than one work by the same author within parentheses in the text, keyed to an alphabetical list of sources on a "Works Cited" page at the end of the paper, as well as notes (footnotes or endnotes). See *The MLA Style Manual* and *The MLA Handbook for Writers of Research Papers*, particularly Citation and bibliography format.
- The MHRA Style Guide is published by the Modern Humanities Research Association (MHRA) and most widely used in the arts and humanities in the United Kingdom, where the MHRA is based. It is available for sale both in the UK and in the United States. It is similar to MLA style, but has some differences. For example, MHRA style uses footnotes that reference a citation fully while also providing a bibliography. Some readers find it advantageous that the footnotes provide full citations, instead of shortened references, so that they do not need to consult the bibliography while reading for the rest of the publication details.

Law

- The Bluebook is a citation system traditionally used in American academic legal writing, and the Bluebook (or similar systems derived from it) are used by many courts. At present, academic legal articles are always footnoted, but motions submitted to courts and court opinions traditionally use inline citations which are either separate sentences or separate clauses.

- The legal citation style used almost universally in Canada is based on the *Canadian Guide to Uniform Legal Citation* (aka *McGill Guide*), published by *McGill Law Journal.*

Sciences, Mathematics, Engineering, Physiology, and Medicine

- The American Chemical Society style, or ACS style, is often used in chemistry and other physical sciences. In ACS style references are numbered in the text and in the reference list, and numbers are repeated throughout the text as needed.
- In the style of the American Institute of Physics (AIP style), references are also numbered in the text and in the reference list, with numbers repeated throughout the text as needed.
- Styles developed for the American Mathematical Society (AMS), or AMS styles, such as AMS-LaTeX, are typically implemented using the BibTeX tool in the LaTeX typesetting environment. Brackets with author's initials and year are inserted in the text and at the beginning of the reference. Typical citations are listed in-line with alphabetic-label format, e.g. [AB90]. This type of style is also called a *"Authorship trigraph."*
- The Vancouver system, recommended by the Council of Science Editors (CSE), is used in medical and scientific papers and research.

- In one major variant, that used by the American Society of Mechanical Engineers (AME), citation numbers are included in the text in square brackets rather than as superscripts. All bibliographical information is exclusively included in the list of references at the end of the document, next to the respective citation number.
- The International Committee of Medical Journal Editors (ICMJE) is reportedly the original kernel of this biomedical style which evolved from the Vancouver 1978 editors' meeting. The MEDLINE/ PubMed database uses this citation style and the National Library of Medicine provides "ICMJE Uniform Requirements for Manuscripts Submitted to Biomedical Journals — Sample References".

- The style of the Institute of Electrical and Electronics Engineers (IEEE), or IEEE style, encloses citation numbers within square brackets and arranges the reference list by the order of citation, not by alphabetical order.
- Pechenik Citation Style is a style described in *A Short Guide to Writing about Biology*, 6th ed. (2007), by Jan A. Pechenik.
- In 2006, Eugene Garfield proposed a bibliographic system for scientific literature, to consolidate the integrity of scientific publications.

Social Sciences

- The style of the American Psychological Association, or APA style, published in *The Style Manual of the APA*, is most often used in social sciences. APA style uses Harvard referencing within the text, listing the author's name and year of publication, keyed to an alphabetical list of sources at the end of the paper on a References page

- The American Political Science Association publishes both a style manual and a style guide for publications in this field.
- The American Anthropological Association utilizes a modified form of the Chicago Style laid out in their Publishing Style Guide

Citation Index

First it is pertinent to note that citation index is an index of citations between publications, allowing the user to easily establish which later documents cite which earlier documents. The first citation indices were legal citators such as Shepard's Citations (1873). In 1960, Eugene Garfield's Institute for Scientific Information (ISI) introduced the first citation index for papers published in academic journals, starting with the *Science Citation Index* (SCI), and later expanding to produce the *Social Sciences Citation Index* (SSCI) and the *Arts and Humanities Citation Index* (AHCI). As of 2006, there are other sources of such data, such as Google Scholar.

There are two publishers of general-purpose academic citation indexes, available to libraries by subscription:

(a) ISI is now part of Thomson Scientific. Though the ISI citation indexes are still published in print and compact disc, they are now generally accessed through the Web under the name *Web of Science,* which is in turn part of the group of databases in *WoK.*

(b) Elsevier publishes Scopus, available online only, which similarly combines subject searching with citation browsing and tracking in the sciences and social sciences.

There are a number of other indexes, more readily available. Some of the currently notable ones are:

(a) The CiteSeerX system provides citation and other searching of scientific literature, primarily in the fields of computer and information science

(b) RePec provides this in economics, and other discipline-specific indexes have also begun to include it in their indexes. Even journal publishers often supply the facility to link to late citations, at least from the journals they publish.

(c) Google Scholar (GS) has citation functionality, limited to the recent articles that are included. There is already discussion about the possibility that GS may in the future have sufficient capabilities to make the commercial products unnecessary.

Each of these products offer an index of citations between publications and a mechanism to establish which documents cite which other documents. The different products offer different ways to access the citation list and also display their citation index differently. They differ widely in cost: WOK and Scopus are among the highest-cost subscription databases; the others mentioned are free.

Citation Analysis

While citation indexes were originally designed for information retrieval purposes, they are increasingly used for bibliometrics and other studies involving research evaluation. Citation data is also the basis of the popular journal impact factor.

There is large body of literature on citation analysis, sometimes called scientometrics, a term invented by Vasily Nalimov, or more specifically bibliometrics. The field blossomed with the advent of the Science Citation Index, which now covers source literature from 1900 on. The leading journals of the field are Scientometrics *and the* Journal of the American Society of Information Science and Technology. *ASIST also hosts an electronic mailing list called SIGMETRICS at ASIST. This method is undergoing a resurgence based on the wide dissemination of the Web of Science and Scopus subscription databases in many universities, and the universally-available free citation tools such as CiteBase, CiteSeerX, Google Scholar, and Windows Live Academic.*

In a classic 1965 paper, Derek J. de Solla Price described the inherent linking characteristic of the SCI as "Networks of Scientific Papers". The links between citing and cited papers became dynamic when the SCI began to be published online. The Social Sciences Citation Index became one of the first databases to be mounted on the Dialog system in 1972. With the advent of the CD-ROM edition, linking became even easier and enabled the use of bibliographic coupling (M. M. Kessler) for finding related records. In 1973 Henry Small published his classic work on Co-Citation analysis which became a self-organizing classification system that led to document clustering experiments and eventually an Atlas of Science later called Research Reviews.

ISI also published Current Contents, a paper publication reproducing journal title pages, widely used at the time for keeping up with the current literature, a technique known as selective dissemination of information (SDI), periodic updates of literature searches based on user profiles. The combination with SCI permitted the first use in 1965 of earlier cited references as a factor in the selection, in a product called Automatic Subject Citation Alert. This continues in electronic form as the ISI Personal Alert; this feature is now almost universally available in any bibliometric database and for most electronic journals. In the case of SCI/SSCI profiles contained not only traditional natural language search terms, but also terms for cited references and cited authors, though this too is now a part of most such systems. Thus, a user can be alerted to any new works which cited the author, paper or book in question. Using journal names in a similar way, customized contents pages could also be provided.

The inherent topological and graphical nature of the worldwide citation network which is an inherent property of the scientific literature was described by Ralph Garner at Drexel University in 1965.

The use of citation counts to rank journals was a technique used in the early part of the nineteenth century but the systematic ongoing measurement of ths counts for scientific journals was initiated by Eugene Garfield at the Institute for Scientific Information who also pioneered the use of these counts to rank authors and papers. In a landmark paper of 1965 he and Irving Sher showed the correlation between citation frequency and eminence in demonstrating that Nobel Prize winners published five times the average number of papers while their work was cited 30 to 50 times the average. In a long series of essays on the Nobel and other prizes Garfield reported this phenomenon. The usual summary measure is known as impact factor, the number of citations to a journal for the previous two years, divided by the number of articles published in those years. It is widely used, both for appropriate and inappropriate purposes—in particular, the use of this measure alone for ranking authors and papers is therefore quite controversial.

In an early study in 1964 of the use of Citation Analysis in writing the history of DNA, Garfield and Sher demonstrated the potential for generating historiographs, topological maps of the most important steps in the history of scientific topics. This work was later automated by E. Garfield, A. I. Pudovkin of the Institute of Marine Biology, Russian Academy of Sciences and V. S. Istomin of Center for Teaching, Learning, and Technology, Washington State University and led to the creation of the HistCite software around 2002. Autonomous citation indexing was introduced in 1998 by Giles, Lawrence and Bollacker and enabled automatic algorithmic extraction and grouping of citations for any digital academic and scientific document. Where previous citation extraction was a manual process, citation measures could now be computed for any scholarly and scientific field and document venue, not just those selected by organizations such as ISI. This led to the creation of new systems for public and automated citation indexing, the first being CiteSeer (now CiteSeerX, soon followed by Cora (recently reborn as Rexa), which focused primarily on the field of computer and information science. These were later followed by large scale academic domain citation systems such as the Google Scholar and previously Microsoft Academic. Such autonomous citation indexing is not yet perfect in citation extraction or citation clustering with an error rate estimated by some at 10% though a careful statistical sampling has yet to be done. This has resulted in such authors as Ann Arbor, Milton Keynes, and Walton Hall being credited with extensive academic output. It should be noted that SCI claims to create automatic citation indexing through purely programmatic methods and even the older records have a similar magnitude of error.

ACCESSION NUMBER

An accession number is a sequential number given to each new book, magazine subscription, or recording as it is entered in the catalog of a library. If an item is removed from the collection, its number is usually not reused for new items. This numbering system is usually in addition to the library classification number (or alphanumeric code) and to the ISBN or International Standard Book Number assigned by publishers.

Accession numbers are also used by museums to identify objects by the order in which they entered the museum's collection. In many museums, the accession number will consist of the year acquired and a sequential number separated by a period. In addition, departments or art classifications within the museum may reserve sections of numbers. For example, objects identified by the numbers 11.300 through 11.350 may indicate objects obtained by the museum in 1911; the first 299 numbers may be used to indicate American art, while the next fifty (11.300-350) may be used for African art.

CUTTER EXPANSIVE CLASSIFICATION

> "No one, perhaps, can remember it all; it cannot be learned, even in part, very quickly; but those who use the library much will find that they become familiar in time unconsciously with all that they have much occasion to use."
>
> —*How to Get Books by C.A. Cutter, (1882)*

Charles Ammi Cutter (1837–1903), inspired by the decimal classification of his contemporary Melvil Dewey, originally developed his own classification scheme for the collections of the Boston Athenaeum, at which he served as librarian for two dozen years. He began work on it about 1880 and published the first schedules in the early 1890s. His five-volume catalogue of the Athenaeum collection is a classic in bibliographic history.

The Cutter classification, although adopted by comparatively few libraries, mostly in New England, has been called one of the most logical and scholarly of American classifications. Its outline served as a basis for the Library of Congress classification, which also took over some of its features. It did not catch on as did Dewey's system because Cutter died before it was completely finished, making no provision for the kind of development necessary as the bounds of knowledge expanded and scholarly emphases changed throughout the 20th century.

Like the LC classification system, texts are organized by subject. Users of Cutter, however, will find the subject headings more general than those of the LC system.

- A General works (encyclopedias, periodicals, society publications)
- B–D Philosophy, Psychology, Religion
- E, F, G Biography, History, Geography and travels
- H–J, K Social sciences, Law
- L–T Science and technology
- U–VS Military, Sports, Recreation
- VT, VV, W Theatre, Music, Fine arts
- X Philology (expanded by language)
- Y Literature (expanded by language, and in English form—e.g., YY is English and American literature, YYP is poetry in English)
- Z Book arts, Bibliography

Constructing Cutter Call Numbers

Most call numbers in the Cutter classification follow conventions offering clues to the book's subject. The first line represents the subject, the second the author (and perhaps title), the third and fourth dates of editions, indications of translations, and critical works on particular books or authors.

All numbers in the Cutter system are (or should be) shelved as if in decimal order.

Size of volumes is indicated by points (.), pluses (+), or slashes (/ or //).

For some subjects a numerical geographical subdivision follows the classification letters on the first line. The number 83 stands for the United States—hence, F83 is U.S. history, G83 U.S. travel, JU83 U.S. politics, WP83 U.S. painting. Geographical numbers are often further expanded decimally to represent more specific areas, sometimes followed by a capital letter indicating a particular city.

The second line usually represents the author's name by a capital letter plus one or more numbers arranged decimally. This may be followed by the first letter or letters of the title in lower-case, and/or sometimes the letters a,b,c indicating other printings of the same title. When appropriate, the second line may begin with a 'form' number—e.g., 1 stands for history and criticism of a subject, 2 for a bibliography, 5 for a dictionary, 6 for an atlas or maps, 7 for a periodical, 8 for a society or university publication, 9 for a collection of works by different authors.

On the third line a capital Y indicates a work about the author or book represented by the first two lines, and a capital E (for English—other letters are used for other languages) indicates a translation into English. If both criticism and translation apply to a single title, the number expands into four lines.

Cutter Numbers

One of the features adopted by other systems, including Library of Congress, is the Cutter number. It is an alphanumeric device to code text so that it can be arranged in alphabetical order using the least amount of characters. It contains one or two initial letters and Arabic numbers, treated as a decimal. To construct a Cutter number, a cataloguer consults a Cutter table as required by the classification rules. Although Cutter numbers are mostly used for coding the names of authors, the system can be used for titles, subjects, geographic areas, and more.

- Bliss, Henry Evelyn. *The Organization of Knowledge in Libraries: and the Subject-Approach to Books*, 2nd ed. New York: H.W. Wilson, 1939.
- Cutter, Charles A. *Rules for a Dictionary Catalog*. W. P. Cutter, ed. 4th ed. Washington, D.C.: Government Printing Office, 1904. London: The Library Association, 1962.
- Cutter, William Parker. *Charles Ammi Cutter*. Chicago: American Library Association, 1931. Ann Arbor, MI: University Microfilms, 1969.
- Foster, William E. "Charles Ammi Cutter: A Memorial Sketch". *Library Journal* 28 (1903): 697-704.
- Immroth, John Philip. "Cutter, Charles Ammi". *Encyclopedia of Library and Information Science*. Allen Kent and Harold Lancour, ed. 47 vols. New York, M. Dekker [1968-].

REFERENCES

Bliss, Henry E. (1910). A modern classification for libraries, with simple notation, mnemonics, and alternatives. *Library Journal* 35, 351–358.

Bliss, Henry E. (1935). *A system of bibliographic classification*. New York: H.W. Wilson.

Bliss, Henry E. (1940-1953). *A bibliographic classification, extended by systematic auxiliary schedules for composite specification* (4 volumes). New York: H.W. Wilson.

Chan, Lois Mai. *Cataloging and Classification: An Introduction.* New York: McGraw-Hill, 1994.

DDC Dewey Decimal Classification : proposed revision of 780 music / prepared under the direction of Russell Sweeney and John Clews with assistance from Winton E. Mathews, Jr. Albany N.Y. : Forest Press, 1980.

Internet Archive: Details: The British Catalogue Of Music 1960.

Maltby, Arthur & Gill, Lindy (1979). *The case for Bliss.* London: Clive Bingley.

Morelon, Régis & Roshdi Rashed (1996), Encyclopedia of the History of Arabic Science, vol. 3, Routledge.

The British Catalogue of Music Classification / compiled for the Council of the British National Bibliography Ltd. by E.J. Coates, F.L.A. London : Council of the British National Bibliography, 1960.

Thomas, Alan R. (1997). Bibliographical classification: the ideas and achievements of Henry E. Bliss. *Cataloging & Classification Quarterly* 25 (1), 51–104.

Svenonius, Elaine. *The Intellectual Foundation of Information Organization.* Cambridge, Mass: MIT Press, 2000.

2

Cataloguing and Indexing

What is Cataloguing?

Library catalogs originated as manuscript lists, arranged by format (folio, quarto, etc.) or in a rough alphabetical arrangement by author. Printed catalogs, sometimes called dictionary catalogs enabled scholars outside a library to gain an idea of its contents. These would sometimes be interleaved with blank leaves on which additions could be recorded, or bound as guardbooks in which slips of paper were bound in for new entries. Slips could also be kept loose in cardboard or tin boxes, stored on shelves. The first card catalogs appeared in the nineteenth century, enabling much more flexibility, and towards the end of the twentieth century the OPAC was developed.

(a) c. 800: Library catalogues are introduced in the House of Wisdom and other medieval Islamic libraries where books are organized into specific genres and categories.

(b) 1595: *Nomenclator* of Leiden University Library appears, the first printed catalog of an institutional library.

(c) 1674: Thomas Hyde's catalog for the Bodleian Library.

Basically, a library catalogue is a register of all bibliographic items found in a library or group of libraries, such as a network of libraries at several locations. A bibliographic item can be any information entity (e.g., books, computer files, graphics, realia, cartographic materials, etc.), that is considered library material (e.g., a single novel in an anthology), or a group of library materials (e.g., a trilogy), or linked from the catalog (e.g., a webpage) as far as it is relevant to the catalog and to the users (patrons) of the library.

The card catalog was a familiar sight to library users for generations, but it has been effectively replaced by the online public access catalog (OPAC). Some still refer to the online catalog as a "card catalog." Some libraries with OPAC access still have card catalogs on site, but these are now strictly a secondary resource and are seldom updated. Many of the libraries that have retained their physical card catalog post a sign advising the last year that the card catalog was updated. Some libraries have eliminated their card catalog in favour of the OPAC for the purpose of saving space for other use, such as additional shelving.

Charles Ammi Cutter made the first explicit statement regarding the objectives of a bibliographic system in his Rules for a Printed Dictionary Catalog in 1876.

According to Cutter, those objectives were

1. to enable a person to find a book of which either (Identifying objective)
   - the author
   - the title
   - the subject

is known.

2. to show what the library has (Collocating objective)
   - by a given author

- on a given subject
- in a given kind of literature

3. to assist in the choice of a book (Evaluating objective)
   - as to its edition (bibliographically)
   - as to its character (literary or topical)

These objectives can still be recognized in more modern definitions formulated throughout the 20th century. 1960/61 Cutter's objectives were revised by Lubetzky and Lubetzky and the Conference on Cataloging Principles (CCP) in Paris. The latest attempt to describe a library catalog's goals and functions was made in 1998 with Functional Requirements for Bibliographic Records (FRBR) which defines four user tasks: find, identify, select, and obtain.

Categories

Traditionally, there are the following types of catalog:

(1) *Author* catalog: a formal catalog, sorted alphabetically according to the authors' or editors' names of the entries.

(2) *Title* catalog: a formal catalog, sorted alphabetically according to the title of the entries.

(3) *Dictionary* catalog: a catalog in which all entries (author, title, subject, series) are interfiled in a single alphabetical order. This was the primary form of card catalog in the Anglo-American world just prior to the introduction of the computer-based catalog.

(4) *Keyword* catalog: a subject catalog, sorted alphabetically according to some system of keywords.

(5) Mixed alphabetic catalog forms: sometimes, one finds a mixed author / title, or an author / title / keyword catalog.

(6) *Systematic* catalog: a subject catalog, sorted according to some systematic subdivision of subjects. Also called a *Classified* catalog.

(7) *Shelf list* catalog: a formal catalog with entries sorted in the same order as bibliographic items are shelved. This catalog may also serve as the primary inventory for the library.

Cataloging Rules

Cataloging (or cataloguing) rules have been defined to allow for consistent cataloging of various library materials across several persons of a cataloging team and across time. Users can use them to clarify how to find an entry and how to interpret the data in an entry. Cataloging rules prescribe

(a) which information from a bibliographic item is included in the entry;

(b) how this information is presented on a catalog card or in a cataloging record;

(c) how the entries should be sorted in the catalog.

The larger a collection, the more elaborate cataloging rules are needed. Users cannot and do not want to examine hundreds of catalog entries or even dozens of library items to find the one item they need. Currently, most cataloging rules are similar to, or even based on, the International Standard Bibliographic Description (ISBD), a set of rules produced by the International Federation of Library Associations and Institutions (IFLA) to describe a wide range of library materials. These rules organize the bibliographic description of an item in the following areas: title and statement of responsibility (author or editor), edition, material-dependent information (for example, the scale of a map), publication and distribution, physical description (for example, number of pages), series, notes, and standard number (ISBN). The most commonly used set of cataloging rules in the English speaking world are the Anglo-American Cataloguing Rules, 2nd Edition, or AACR2 for short. In the German-speaking world there exists the *Regeln für die alphabetische Katalogisierung,* abbreviated RAK. AACR2 has been translated into many languages, however, for use around the world. AACR2 provides rules for *descriptive cataloging* only and does not touch upon *subject cataloging.*

In fact, Library items that are written in a foreign script are, in some cases, transliterated to the script of the catalog.

Sorting

In a title catalog, one can distinguish two sort orders:

1. In the *grammatical* sort order (used mainly in older catalogs), the most important word of the title is the first sort term. The importance of a word is measured by grammatical rules; for example, the first noun may be defined to be the most important word.
2. In the *mechanical* sort order, the first word of the title is the first sort term. Most new catalogs use this scheme, but still include a trace of the grammatical sort order: they neglect an article (The, A, etc.) at the beginning of the title.

The grammatical sort order has the advantage that often, the most important word of the title is also a good keyword (question 3), and it is the word most users remember first when their memory is incomplete. However, it has the disadvantage that many elaborate grammatical rules are needed, so that only expert users may be able to search the catalog without help from a librarian. In some catalogs, person's names are standardized, i.e., the name of the person is always (cataloged and) sorted in a standard form, even if it appears differently in the library material. This standardization is achieved by a process called authority control. An advantage of the authority control is that it is easier to answer question 2 (which works of some author does the library have?). On the other hand, it may be more difficult to answer question 1 (does the library have some specific material?) if the material spells the author in a peculiar variant. For the cataloger, it may incur (too) much work to check whether *Smith, J.* is *Smith, John* or *Smith, James*.

For some works, even the title can be standardized. The technical term for this is *uniform title*. For example, translations and reeditions are sometimes sorted under their original title. In many catalogs, parts of the Bible are sorted under the standard name of the book(s) they contain. The plays of William Shakespeare are another frequently cited example of the role played by a *uniform title* in the library catalog.

Technically, many complications about alphabetic sorting of entries arise. Some examples:

1. Some languages know sorting conventions that differ from the language of the catalog. For example, some Dutch catalogs sort *IJ* as *Y*. Should an English catalog follow this suit? And should a Dutch catalog sort non-Dutch words the same way?
2. Some titles contain numbers, for example *2001: A Space Odyssey*. Should they be sorted as numbers, or spelled out as *Two thousand and one*?
3. *de Balzac, Honoré* or *Balzac, Honoré de*? *Ortega y Gasset, José* or *Gasset, José Ortega y*?

For a fuller discussion, see collation.

In a subject catalog, one has to decide on which

classification system to use. The cataloger will select appropriate subject headings for the bibliographic item and a unique classification number (sometimes known as a "call number") which is used not only for identification but also for the purposes of shelving, placing items with similar subjects near one another, which aids in browsing by library users, who are thus often able to take advantage of serendipity in their search process.

Online Catalogues

Online cataloging has greatly enhanced the usability of catalogs, thanks to the rise of MAchine Readable Cataloging = MARC standards in the 1960s. Rules governing the creation of catalog MARC records include not only formal cataloging rules like AACR2 but also special rules specific to MARC, available from the Library of Congress and also OCLC. MARC was originally used to automate the creation of physical catalog cards; Now the MARC computer files are accessed directly in the search process. OPACs have enhanced usability over traditional card formats because:

1. The online catalog does not need to be sorted statically; the user can choose author, title, keyword, or systematic order dynamically.
2. Most online catalogs offer a search facility for any word of the title; the goal of the grammatic word order (provide an entry on the word that most users would look for) is reached even better.
3. Many online catalogs allow links between several variants of an author name. So, authors can be found both under the original and the standardised name (if entered properly by the cataloguer).
4. The elimination of paper cards has made the information more accessible to many people with

disabilities, such as the visually impaired, wheelchair bound, and those who suffer from mold allergies.

It has been so far amply demonstrated that computers can successfully be used as an aid to "cataloguing". The Ohio College Library Centre (OCLC), in fact, now provides an on-line cataloguing service in North America. It is less expensive and far more efficient than its participants can provide for themselves. In India, such a system does not exist. In fact, it is not economically feasible at present to have such a network in India for reasons such as:

1. Lack of telecommunication facilities; because of our insufficient telecommunication system, it is not economically feasible to have links (through dedicated cables) with international systems (like, OCLC)
2. Non-availability of bibliographies (such as, national bibliography) in a machine-readable form; even if they are in the machine-readable form, they may have very little use(for the purpose of cataloguing) since most of our libraries (especially academic and research libraries) acquire mainly foreign publications.

Under these circumstances, libraries in India must think of developing their own automated cataloguing systems. It can be developed easily as a by-product of a book-ordering system. If a few libraries in a region develop automated cataloguing systems, a library network similar to that of the OCLC may be possible in the near future.

The main activity of cataloguing systems is the production of catalogue cards. Because of the availability of high-speed printers, book catalogues are becoming extremely popular. In recent years, catalogues in microfiche are becoming very popular since they are least expensive and more durable than book catalogues. In a computer-aided cataloguing system, we can also produce, as a by-product of it, spine labels, book pockets and book cards for use in circulation systems. Also it further helps us to provide most economically cataloguing information to branch libraries. Procedures involved in cataloguing are:

1. Preparing worksheets.
2. Generating machine-readable records consisting of appropriate tags; these records can either be on punch cards or they can be stored directly on tape or disk (through terminals)
3. Verification of the machine-readable catalogues (CORC); it is usually on tape and key to the record is preferably through the call number.
4. Generation of added entries (such as author entry, title entry, series entry, etc.). These entries can be stored in a file called "inverted file". In this file, the records consist of data elements and the link to the main record in the CORC; the data element may be either author or title, or any other item which is in the main entry.
5. Generation of indexes and cross-reference entries. Records of the index files can be merged appropriately into the inverted file and the records of the cross-reference files can also be merged appropriately into the CORC. To generate indexes and cross-reference entries, it is essential to maintain a subject authority file.
6. Printing the records (from both the CORC and the inverted file) in card form, or in book form or in machine-readable form.

Cataloguing Using Unit Record Machines

To develop an automated cataloguing system, we can use either unit record machines or general purpose digital computers. In unit record systems, cataloguing information is keypunched and the resulting punched cards are sorted into a desired filing sequence using sorters. Sorted cards are then processed using the tabulators to obtain either book catalogues or card catalogues. Tabulators may also be used to obtain added entries on punched cards. These punched cards have to be sorted again using the sorter to obtain a printed list. However, for a large library, use of unit record machines is prohibitive due to:

(1) Difficulties in handling large files of punched cards,

(2) Non-availability of lower case letters, diacritics, etc., in the unit record machines,

(3) Limited number of characters that can be punched in the unit record (i.e., punch card).

(4) Difficulties in arranging the records in a desired sequence.

Despite these limitations, a large number of book catalogues were produced in the 1940s by many libraries using unit record machines.

Machine Readable Catalogues (MARC)

Among the developments of MARC, the most important development is the programme of the Library of Congress for distribution of catalogue data in tape form. From these tapes, any library in the world can economically acquire machine-readable catalogue data, just as it has been able to acquire catalogue cards. The basic machine readable catalogue record on a MARC tape consists of the Leader, the Record Directory, the Control Fields and the Variable fields.

Leader	Record Directory	Control Fields	Variable Fields

The control field consists of both variable control number and Variable fixed Fields. The leader is fixed in length for all records contains 24 characters. It is a set of fields describing the general structure of the individual entry. The Record Directory is an index to the location of the Control and Variable Fields in the record. It consists of a series of fixed length entries, one for each variable field in the record.

An entry in the Record Directory contains the identification tag, the length and starting character position in the record of each of the Variable Field. The Record Directory will end with a field-terminator code. Since the number of variable fields in a record can vary, the total length of the record directory is also variable. Variable Fields (including the control fields) are made up of variable length alphanumeric data. All fields end with a field terminator code, except the last variable field in a logical record which replaces the field-terminator with an end of record code. Each variable field is identified by a three character numeric tag in the record directory. Tags may be repeated as required in a logical record. However, tags associated with the control fields will not be repeated in a logical record.

A detailed outline of Leader, Directory, Control Fields and Variable Fields is given below:

A Leader
Record length
Control Fields
Variable Fields

Description of the Data Elements: The total number of characters in the leader is 24, and there are nine data elements in the leader. They are given in Table 16.10. Data elements for the record directory are given in Table 16.11. There are actually three data elements (tag, field length and starting character position) in each field. The number of fields in the directory is exactly equivalent to the number of data fields (both control fields and variable fields) in the record Data elements for the control fields.

As has been pointed out earlier, a variable field consists of indicators, subfield codes, data elements and the field terminator. Further, each variable field is assigned a tag and the tag is stored in the directory. These are briefly discussed below.

The directory, control fields and the variable fields are always terminated by a *Field Terminator*. Finally the last character in the record is a *Record Terminator*. Indicators: Each variable field will begin with 2 character code which provides descriptive information about the field. The contents of the indicators are specified for the fields in which they are used.

Data Elements in the Leader of a MARC Record

Element Number	*Name of the Data Elements*	*Number of characters*	*Remarks*
1	Logical record length (0-4)	5	The total number of characters in the logical record including itself. The number is right justified with leading zeros.
2	Record status (5)	1	n=New record, c=Corrected/revised record, d=Deleted records.
3	Type of Record (6)	1	a = Language material printed, etc.
4	Bibliographic level (7)	1	m = Monograph, a = Analytical, c = Collection
5	Blank characters (8-9)	2	For local purposes
6	Indicator count (10)	1	Each variable field begins with two characters called indicators which provide certain descriptive information

			about the data which follows. For monographs all variable fields must be incremented by 2 to reach the subfield code for the first data element in the field.
7	Subfield code count (11)	1	Each data element within a variable field is identified by a two character subfield code made up of a delimiter ($) and a lower case alphabetic character. Each data element must be incremented by 2 in order to reach the first character of data.
8	Base address of data (12-16)	5	A number which is the starting character position of the first control field. That is, it is equal to the length of the leader and the record directory (including the record directory field terminator). The starting character position for each field entered in the record is relative to the first character of the first control field (not the beginning of the record). The number is right justified with leading zeros.
9	Blank characters (17-25)	7	For local use.

Note: In the 2nd column, the number in the parentheses refers to the position of the data element in the Leader.

Data Elements in the Record Directory of a MARC Record.

Element Number	*Name of the Data elements*	*Number of characters*	*Character position in the directory*
1	Tag	3	0-2
2	Field length	4	3-6
3	Starting character position	5	7-11

Notes: 1. Tag is a 3 character number which identifies the field.

2. Field length is the number of characters in the field identified by the tag. This count includes indicators, subfield codes, data, and field terminator. The number is right justified with leading zeros.

3. All suffixes to the LC card number are carried as variable length data. This data does not affect the uniqueness of the LC card number. It is possible to determine the presence

and/or length of the suffix by subtracting 12 from the total length of field 001.

4. For more details regarding the data elements for TAG 008. MARC manual of the library of Congress may be referred to.

Control Field Description in MARC

Tag	*Name of the control field*		*Data Elements*	*No. of characters*	*Character position in the field*
001	Library of	1	Alphabetic Prefix	3	0-2
	Congress	2	Year	2	3-4
	card number	3	Number	6	5-10
	(control	4	Supplement	1	11
	number)	5	Suffix	Variable	12
008	Fixed length	1	Data entered on file	6	0-5
	data	2	Type of publication data code	1	6
	elements	3	Date 1	4	7-10
		4	Date 2	4	11-14
		5	Country of publication code	3	15-17
		6	Illustration code	4	18-21
		7	Intellectual level code	1	22
		8	Form of reproduction code	1	23
		9	Form of content codes	4	24-27
		10	Govt. Pub. indicator	1	28
		11	Conference or meeting indicator	1	29
		12	Festichrift indicator	1	30
		13	Index indicator	1	31
		14	Main entry in body of entry indicator	1	32
		15	Fiction indicator	1	33
		16	Biography code	1	34
		17	Language code	3	35-37
		18	Modified record indicator	1	38
		19	Cataloguing service code	1	39

Note: 1. The alphabetic prefix is left justified with blank fill, and if no prefix is present, there will be 3 blanks before the numeric portion of the number. The six digit identification number is right justified with zero fill.

Example: A 66-11 = ABB 66 0 0 0 0 11

Ac66-111 = A C bbb 0 0 0 111

68-4897 = *B B B* 68 0 04897

2. Starting character position is a 5-character number. It gives the character position in the record of the first character of the field.
3. Example: (a) 001 0014 00000

   (b) 008 0047 00014

   (c) 001 0058 00061
4. In a variable field, the first actual data character is the fifth character, i.e., the starting character position plus 4.

Subfield Codes: Variable fields are made up of a single data elements or a group of data elements. The subfield code precedes each data element in a field and identifies the data element. The subfield code consists of 2 characters. For the purpose of these specifications, the delimiter will be represented by "$", Subfield codes are discussed in detail in the MARC Manual.

Data Elements.: All the data elements in the variable fields may have variable lengths.

Variable Field Tags: All variable field tags may be repeated; however, the nature of cataloguing data is such that many tags are not repeatable, e.g. a record for a monograph can only have one main entry and, therefore, only one field in the 100 series.

Subfield Codes in Variable Fields: The subfield code identifies the constituent data elements of a variable field. For example, the *imprint* field, tag 260, may have the following 3 data elements in its respective subfield codes:

Place $a
Publisher $b
Date $c

Imprint data could appear as follows with hypothetical record directory entries and indicators carrying blanks:

Directory: 26 000 45 2 0 8

Data: BB a New Delhi $ b Wiley-Eastern

Directory: 26 000 48 0 2 8

Data : BB$a London $a New York $b Macmillan, $c 1965$c1964

Variable Field Tags

Tag	*Data Elements*
	Control Numbers
*010	LC card number
*011	Linking LC card number
*015	National bibliography number
*016	Linking NBN
*020	Standard book number
*021	linking SBN
*025	Overseas acquisitions number (PL 480, Lacap, etc.)
*026	Linking OAN number
*035	Local system number
*036	Linking local system number
*040	Cataloguing source
*041	languages
*042	Search Code
	Knowledge Numbers
050	LC call number
051	Copy statement
060	NLM call number

070		NAL call number
*071		NAL subject category number
*080		UDC number
*081		BNB classification number
082		Dewey decimal classification Number
*090		Local call number
	Main Entry	
100		Personal name
110		Corporate name
111		Conference or meeting
130		Uniform title heading
	Supplied Titles	
240		Uniform title
241		Romanised title
*242		Translated title
	Title Paragraph	
245		Title
250		Edition statement
260		Imprint
	Collation	
300		Collation
350		Bibliographic price
*360		Converted price
	Series Notes	
400		Personal name-title (Traced name)
410		Corporate name-title (Traced name)
	Series Notes	
411		Conference-title (Traced name)
440		Title (Traced name)
490		Series untraced or traced differently
	Bibliographic Notes	
500		General notes
501	*"Bound with" note*	
502		Dissertation note
503		Bibliographic history note
504		Bibliography note

505		Contents note (formatted)
*506		"Limited Use" note
520		Abstract or annotation
	Subject Added Entries	
600		Personal name
610		Corporate name (excluding political jurisdiction alone)
611		Conference or meeting
630		Uniform title heading
	LC Subject Headings	
650		Topical
651		Geographic names
652		Political jurisdictions alone or with subject sub-divisions
	Other Subject headings	
*660		NLM subject heading (MESH)
*670		NAL subject headings
*690		Local subject heading systems
	Other Added Entries	
700		Personal name
710		Corporate name
711		Conference or meeting
730		Uniform title heading
740		Title traced differently
750		Name not capable of authorship
	Series Added Entries	
800		Personal name-title
810		Corporate name-title
811		Conference or meeting title
840		Title

*The Library of Congress will not supply data for these fields.

Cataloguing has been a traditional art and science of librarianship. The development of computer and communication technologies has contributed towards standardisation of the entry format and the cataloguing system at international, national and local levels.

The drudgery in developing local catalogues and making them compatible for resource sharing with other libraries has been eliminated due to the development of machine-readable cataloguing system. Therefore, it is imperative on the part of librarians to adopt information technology for efficient access to documents and their information contents. There are several international standards for Machine-Readable Bibliographic Records. Some of them are:

1. Standard for Record Structure (ISO 2709)
2. Standard for Coded Character Sets (ISO, 2202 and 2375)
3. Standard for Abbreviation of Periodical Titles (ISO 4)
4. Standard for Form of Calendar Dates in Numeric Form (ISO 2014)
5. Standard for names of Countries (ISO 3166)
6. Standard for Serial Numbering.

Notably, are many other standards related to bibliographic level, language, script, physical medium, role of responsible person or body, etc. Among the various standard, those for the format of bibliographical records are considered as most important because of their applications in information handling. Formats for the bibliographical records may be grouped as:

1. Switching formats
2. Bilateral formats
3. Standard formats

A switching format is used when we would like to switch from one system to another. A bilateral format is designed when two or more institutions agree to use the same format. A standard format may be used for a specific group of users for general use. ISDS (International Serials Data System), AGRIS (International Information for Agricultural Science and TEchnology) and INIS (International Nuclear Information System) record formats are the examples of standard format adopted by a specific group of users. On the other hand, Reference Manual for Bibliographic Descriptions (RMBD, published by UNESCO), universal MARC format (UNIMARC, published by IFLA) and Common Communication Format (CCF, published by UNESCO) are the examples of standard formats designed for general bibliographic use. The RMBD is typically employed by abstracting and indexing organisations; it includes rules for data preparation and it acts as a source for local and bilateral formats. UNIMARC is, however, mainly employed by national libraries to exchange MARC records. It is based on International Standard Bibliographic Description (ISBD). Although, CCF is designed for general bibliographic use, only those data elements which are useful for printed text are included in the standard. It is designed for both local use and for exchange of bibliographic data. Also, it is compatible with UNIMARC and RMBD. It is however, does not include any cataloguing rules and it has a provision to include local data elements. All the three standards (RMBD, UNIMARC and CCF) follow ISO standard for record structure, for coded character sets and for physical tape characteristics.

Indexes are main retrieval tools for any documentation work. Author and subject indexes are accepted as the necessary parts of bibliographical information retrieval systems. The need for subject indexes has arisen mainly due to certain disadvantages of keyword indexes, taxonomic indexes, etc. These indexes quite often retrieve many non relevant documents; precision in retrieval is very less. The concept of keywords and uniterms has thus given rise to a variety of indexes which vary from one another in terms of the vocabulary control used in indexing and in the methods by which they seek to control noise in retrieval.

For quick production of these indexes, computers have been used increasingly since 1950; Which began with Luhn's work on KWIC indexes in 1957. This is primarily because of the fact that routines involved in their productions are easily amenable for mechanisation. Even in this, two distinct levels of attempts are possible.

(a) Merely to use the computer to automate the mechanics of compilation and printing of the hard copy of an index.

(b) To use the computer as an aid in arriving at and printing terms or words considered as suitable for indexing.

An entry in a KWIC index usually consists of one line of text printed in such a way that the particular keyword characterising the entry appears in an alphabetical order in the middle of the line, with both left and right contexts with the corresponding document reference number. The production of KWIC index is a simple mechanised operation consisting of text reading, filtering noise words and automatic sorting routines. The KWIC entries are usually generated from titles of documents; if the titles are not clearly indicative of the content, a KWIC entry will not be much useful in searching.

3

Automation of Library Operations

> "Don't be to worried about these mechnaical brains making man obsolete. Like all other great inventions—from the cigarette machine to TV—they still need somebody standing by to kick them when they refuse to work."

It is pertinent to note that activities related to acquisition of books, classification, cataloguing, book circulation and book maintenance are traditionally known as house-keeping operations. Until recently, these activities were highly labour intensive. In recent times (in India) many librarians are attempting to computerize some of these activities. Depending upon the type of library, we may computerise some of the functions on priority. For example, in a large public library, one may automate circulation control; in a special library, one can computerise serials control; and in an university library, acquisition system may be given priority.

Here we intend to make an attempt to discuss the procedures to computerise some house-keeping operations with the emphasis on design and file requirements.

First of all, we must identify the activities to be automated and then decide on the order of priority in the context of library objectives. For example, if the aim is to have effective control over the serials (especially when we spend about 50 per cent of the total budget allotted for collection development), priority may be given to automating serials control. If the aim is to reduce staff, priority may be given to those areas which are heavily staffed. If the objective is to improve the reader services, we may think of using computers (mainframe/or/mini/micro) to provide additional services and facilities.

Remember, while deciding to take up a project on automation, a question usually arises—is there any guiding principle to proceed with the project?

Remarkably, there are atleast two such principles:

1. The principles of total systems approach
2. The principles of integrated technical processing

Basically, the first principle may suggest taking up a single task/job for automation; by doing so, we may have to face the problem of incompatibility (with the systems to be developed later). Some are of the opinion that a total system must be designed to begin with and, funds permitting, different components of it may be implemented step-by-step at different times. On the other hand, many are of the opinion that a good system design demands elimination of redundancy in inputting as well as in storing the data pertaining to various distinctive library functions. We may, therefore, be guided by the second principle, so as to eliminate the redundancy. In fact some of the largest and most sophisticated systems are based on this principle.

It is, however, interesting to note that the Library of Congress opines that there is a vast difference between acquisition data and cataloguing-data and the use of the former is unlikely to be effectively useful for the latter application. Most of the existing systems follow the first principle and, therefore, we perhaps have several software packages for automation of:

1. Acquisition system
2. Serials control
3. Cataloguing
4. Circulation control.

How to Go Ahead?

Having decided upon the activities to be automated, we must carry out a detailed examination of each activity to:

1. Identify the data elements
2. Calculate the total storage capacity required to:
   (a) ensure that the software (to be acquired/ developed) is able to handle the size, number of fields and the records
   (b) estimate the back-up storage required
   (c) estimate the number of terminals required
3. Identify the various functions to be automated
4. Identify those data elements which are common to several functions.

As general guidelines, the following steps are useful for developing an automated system.

1. Identify various functions of each activity. (For example: IF activity is circulation control, its functions are charging, discharging, renewing, etc.).
2. Identify the input requirements for each of the functions (i.e. data elements)
3. Identify the input in terms of records, files and the media; also determine the size of the files

4. Identify the output required for each of the functions
5. Identify the output in terms of records, files and the media; also determine the size of the files
6. Development of programs (to get the desired output from the given input, using the available hardware) or buying the software/turnkey system to automate certain or all functions of the activities to be automated
7. Implementation and evaluation.

I

ACQUISITION CONTROL

First, we will take the case of acquisition control and its automation in libraries.

Until the 1950s most of the automated acquisition control systems were based on unit record machines. Such a system requires a keypunch, sorter, collator and a tabulating machine (like IBM 402, 403 or 407). In unit record systems, the order information is punched on cards and then they are sorted. Sorted cards are processed using a tabulator to print the orders. A file of outstanding orders can be obtained by collecting the previous orders (which are on cards) with the new one using the collator. This file can also be printed using the tabulator. When the documents are received, the cost price of each document is punched into a corresponding card, which is then used to update financial records, and in some cases to write vouchers. Order files can be processed periodically using the sorter and the tabulator to get the printed list of the books not received. As general purpose computers became widely popular in the 1960s, batch processing systems became the most common and popular form of acquisition system. Most of such systems used punched-cards for inputting order information.

However, the input designs were not greatly different from that of unit record systems; but once the data were fed into the system, information was normally transferred back and forth between magnetic tapes or disc files without the necessity of repeated manual handling of cards.

A typical system of this type, in addition to printing orders, automatically carried out updating of the file of information on orders outstanding and the appropriate financial records storing the bibliographic information for later use. The most popular computers used for acquisition control systems in the mid-1960s were IBM 1400 series, particularly the 1401. The University of Illinois at Chicago began using a 1401 for an off-line acquisition system in 1964. An off-line batch processing system was introduced in 1965 on IBM 1401, at the University of Michigan. Since then, many libraries, introduced such systems in USA and other advanced countries.

By mid-1970s, the cost of on-line storage and the necessary hardware had declined dramatically and by then several on-line systems were in operation in industrially advanced nations. Perhaps, the earliest one was implemented at the Washington State University in 1968. In on-line acquisition systems, each information is tagged; records can be processed directly from the terminals. For instance, it may be edited for valid order number, updated budget information, etc. The objective of the following sections is to highlight the file requirements from the viewpoint of systems design for developing an automated system for book acquisitions. As far as possible, the presentation has been slanted towards the procedures involved in the development of the required software.

Remarkably, during the early period of library automation, many libraries automated their procedures for ordering, receipt and payment of library materials. The early systems were developed with an objective of only order/receipt control or funds accounting; very few systems in fact combined these two functions of acquisitions control. Further, most of the systems were developed using the in-housed, main-frame computers of the libraries' parent organisations. On the other hand, the vendors of the turnkey circulation systems have substantially completed the development of software for their initial products and are now extending their range of services. Also, book-sellers especially those who have in-house computer systems, see significant financial benefits in having libraries submit their orders on-line.

Thus, in recent years, the major initiative in automating acquisitions control comes from the vendors of the automated library systems. The options for automating acquisition control therefore now include not only in-house development but also the purchase of a system or services from a vendor. Because of the many capabilities of automated systems, the acquisitions librarians can effectively handle ordering systems and then can afford to spend sufficient time for collection development and management of funds. Thus, the primary objectives of an automated acquisitions control system are likely to be towards cost containment, speeding up of the receipt of materials, improving fund control, developing single function systems into integrated systems. Before we begin the process of developing or selecting a software to have an automated acquisitions system, we must clearly state the rationale to the process so that decisions can be made quickly and consistently. To begin with, the library administration must examine its motivation in undertaking the project.

Usually, common motivations include:

1. Reducing order back logs
2. Reducing/ containing acquisitions cost

3. Speeding up ordering work (including the receipt of materials)
4. Improving funds control
5. Achieving compatibility (with resource sharing libraries)
6. Move towards integrated systems
7. Committing the library to use the available technology.

Functions of an Automated Acquisitions Control System

An automated acquisitions system is expected to perform certain managerial functions in addition to certain clerical functions (such as pre-order searching, creating purchase order, etc). Systems are usually designed to respond to regular orders, blanket orders, exchanges, etc. It is also designed to handle regular receipt, non-receipt, out of print documents with wrong billing, unwanted documents with right billing, and so on. The typical functions of an automated acquisitions control system are:

(i) Pre-order searching, especially to avoid duplicate orders

(ii) Creating purchase orders:

(a) request for invoice, if necessary

(b) sending order letter (if necessary, along with cheques/drafts)

(iii) Receiving materials:

- (a) Sending cheques/drafts (as and when necessary0
- (b) Completion of accession list
- (c) Announcement of latest documents received
- (d) Completion of cataloguing.

(iv) Claim (for damaged materials) and/or cancellation notices

(v) Providing information to the management (and sometimes to users) on orders outstanding and sometimes on work-in-progress (that is, books received but not yet catalogued)

(vi) Maintaining book fund accounts and printing book fund reports.

In case, there is a delay on the part of the bookseller in supplying a book, the system must prepare a *reminder note.* As and when books are received, it must handle the various associated accounting procedures.

The bibliographic data in the order record can also be amended by the library staff to produce a catalogue card as well as to update the accession list. If a library has a computerised circulation system, the necessary machine-readable book-cards can also be prepared automatically as part of the "Order System". In addition to these, list of orders (by order number, by author, by title, etc.). and various reports of statistical analyses may also be derived from the system. Provision can also be made in the system to perform such functions as:

1. To *hold* orders until funds become available;
2. *To re-orders* from a second vendor if the first cannot supply the documents; and
3. To compute vendor performance measure (e.g., the average time taken to supply books, average discount given, etc.)

Again, the following factors are to be considered in advance while designing an automated acquisitions system:

(i) The files to be maintained

(ii) Data elements in the records of each file

(iii) Record format and media of the file

(iv) Modes of operation (batch processing or on-line).

In a total on-line system, the acquisitions librarian can access the files at any time from his/her desk itself. In a batch processing system, the files are not directly accessible but the printed lists are used. Depending upon the size of the library, the batch processing might be carried out weekly or at some other selected time interval.

To perform the above mentioned functions in a typical system, one may have to maintain at least the following files in machine-readable form:

1. Order file
2. Accession file
3. Fund file

In a batch processing system, these files may be maintained on magnetic tapes. In an on-line system, it is necessary to maintain these files on disks. Data elements constituting the records of each of these files and the record formats are discussed below.

The required data elements for the records may vary from one library to another, depending on the functions to be performed and the capability of the hardware. In brief, the order file contains minimum information required to process an order related to a document and the accession file contains complete information regarding the documents which are available in the library.

In order to have as many data elements as possible in record we can adopt a fixed cum variable field format similar to the MARC format. In such a structure, a record may consist of three parts.

Leader	Directory	Variable Data Fields

Leader

Each record may contain and begin with a 24-character *Leader*. It contains data related to the structure of the record and a few data elements. The data elements in the *Leader* are required primarily to process the record.

TABLE 1

Data Elements in Leader for the Order Record

Character Position	*Name and Description*
0-4	Record length (The total number of characters in the order record)
5	Status code (0=New record: 1=Replacement of a defective copy: 2=Order cancelled: 3=Deleted: etc.) After receiving a document the record status may be changed to "deleted".
6	Type of Document (S=serials, M=monograph, R=report, P=patent, N=non-book material, O=others, etc.)
7	Mode of acquisition (P=purchase, S=subscription. E=exchange, C=complimentary copy, etc.)
8	Reminders sent or not (0=Not sent, 1=Reminder sent).
9	Recorded Level Code (This code may be used to indicate the degree of complexity of the record: for example. 0=the minimum information required to transmit and order such as: ISBN only; the level 0 is effective only in on-line order system. 1-complete information of the document is given: 2=partial information is given along with the ISBN).
10	Length of the field indicators (The number of indicators associated with each variable field: usually it is 2.)
11	Subfield indicator length (The length of the delimiter plus the subfield code used within the fields: it is 0, as no subfields have been suggested here).
12-16	Base address of the data (the sum of the lengths of the

	leader and the directory, including the field terminator at the end of the directory).
17-23	May be used to suit the local needs.

Directory

It is an index to the location of the variable fields within a record. It is made up of a series of fixed length fields consisting of tags, and the starting character position of the field. The directory begins immediately after the *Leader* and ends always with a field terminator. Contents of each field in the directory are given in Table 16.3. The number of entries in the directory depends on the number of the variable data field in the record.

TABLE 2

Data Elements in Leader for the Accession Record

Character Position	*Name and Description*
0-4	Record length *(the total number of characters in the accession record)*
5	*Status code* (0=New record 1=Record has been corrected 2= Document is missing, 3= Document has been weeded out. etc.)
6	Type of document (S=serials, M=monographs, R=report, P=patent. N=non-book materials. O=others, etc.)
7	Mode of Acquisition (P=purchase, S=subscription, E=Exchange, C=Complimentary copy. etc)
8	Location of the document (0=in the main library. A-Z=Branch library code)
9	Blank character (for local use)
10	Length of the field indicators (The number of indicators associated with each variable field: usually it is 2)
11	Subfield indicator length (The length of the delimeter plus the subfield code used within the fields: it is 0, as no subfield has been suggcsted here)

12-16	Base address of the Data (the sum of the lengths of the leader and the directory, including the field terminator at the end of the directory)
17-23	May be used to suit the local needs.

Variable Data Fields

The variable data fields consist of a series of variables (data elements). Each of these fields may begin with the field or subfield indicators. The presence or absence of indicators in the record are indicated (in terms of its length) in the file is printed out usual. The various data elements for an order file or for an Accession File depending on the requirements, are given in the following.

TABLE 3

Data Elements Required for Order Record and Accession Record

Serial No.	*Tag*	*Field indicator*	*Name and Description*
1	001	$a	ISSN
		$b	ISBN
		$c	CODEN
		$d	LC Card No.
		$e	Any other control information
2	002	$a	Accession No.
3	003		*Title associated with*
		$a	Analytic (an article)
		$b	monograph
		$c	Collection
4	004		*Persons associated with*
		$a	Analytic
		$b	Monograph
		$c	Collection
5	005		*Affiliation*
		$a	Analytic
		$b	Monograph
		$c	Collection

6	006		*Corporate body associated with*
		$a	Analytic
		$b	Monograph
		$c	Collection
7	007	$a	Edition
8	008	$a	Volume number
9	009	$a	Part number
10	010	$a	Issue number
11	011		*Date*
		$a	Of publication
		$b	Other than the date of publication
12	012		Language
		$a	of the text
		$b	of the summaries
13	013	$a	Name of publisher
14	014	$a	Place of publication
15	015		Collection
		$a	Analytic
		$b	Monograph
		$c	Collection
			Additional data Elements for Description of Conference Documents
16	016	$a	Name of the meeting
17	017	$a	Location of the meeting
18	018	$a	Date of the meeting
19	019	$a	Identification of patent document
20	020	$a	Persons associated with patent document
21	021	$a	Corporate body associated with patent document
22	022	$a	Domestic filing data of patent document
23	023	$a	Convention priority data of patent document
24	024	$a	Reference to legally related domestic patent document

			Additional Data Elements for Description of Reports
25	025	$a	Report number
26	026	$a	Name of the performing organisation
27	027	$a	Contract/Grant No.
			Additional Data Elements for Description of these and Dissertations.
28	028	$a	University or other educational institutions
29	029	$a	Type of Degree
30	030		*Note*
		$a	Summary only note
		$b	Bibliography note
		$c	Abstract
		$d	Ancillary data
31	031		Subject code
		$a	Broad subject of ordering code
		$b	UDC Number
		$c	CC number
		$d	Other classification number
		$e	Controlled index term
		$f	Uncontrolled index term
32	032	$a	Name of the currency
33	033	$a	Cost/Subscription
34	034		Handling charges
35	035		Exchange rate (for Rs. 100/-)
36	036		Invoice number
37	037		Invoice date
38	038		Invoice amount
39	039		Name of the bank
40	040		Cheque/Draft No.
41	041		Date of the Cheque/Draft
42	042		Binding charge (in local currency)
43	043		*Vendor information*
		$a	Vendor/seller's name

		$b	Person (or the corporate body) with whom the document is exchanged
		$c	Person (or the corporate body) who has given the gift)
44	044	$i	Article (line i) (i=o, 1, 2 **9)
45	045	$a	City
		$b	PIN Code
		$c	Country
46	046		*Dates Related to Order*
47	047	$a	Date when the document is received.
48	048	$a	Date when the document is claimed for a defective copy
49	049		Date when the claimed copy is received
50	050	$a	Date when the order is cancelled
51	051	$a	Date of sending the last reminder
52	052	$a	Date of the approval of the document
53	053	$a	Expected arrival date
54	054	$a	Purchase Order/number
55	055	$a	Quantity ordered
56	056	$a	Missing issue/document information
57	057	$a	Country of publication
58	058	$a	Title of Serieal
59	059	$a	Series designation

Notes:(1) Note all the data elements are necessary for an order file. One has to carefully select the data for an order file (and similarly for an accession file).

(2) Serial Numbers 1 ($a-$e). 10, 56 and 58 are relevant only to serials control system.

(3) For more information regarding the bibliographical data elements, refer to "Reference Manual for Machine Readable Bibliographic Descriptions. Revised Edition 2" Compiled and Edited by H Diericlex and A. Hopkinson. General Information Programme and UNISIST. Unesco. Paris. PGI/81/WS/2

Fund File

Information in the fund file is primarily for the management. It may contain:

(i) Total amount available for the year (in local as well as in foreign currency)

(ii) Amount to be spent for different types of documents (viz. monographs, journals, newspapers/magazines, reports etc.)

(iii) Amount to be spent for different subjects (viz. physics, chemistry, mathematics, etc.)

(iv) Amount spent in the previous months of the current year as suggested in (ii) and (iii).

In fact, we can even store finance data regarding handling charges, postage, etc. for each document. However, such an in-depth analysis may not be really required.

Steps Involved in the Design and Development

In developing the systems, the following steps are involved:

Step A:

Design a worksheet and write the necessary information required for an order in the worksheet.

TABLE 4

A Worksheet to Create In-Process File for Acquisitions System

	Indian Statistical Institute Library Bangalore-560059	
(044)	Order Date:	(054) Order No.
(001)	ISBN:	
(004)	Author:	
(003)	Title:	

(013)	Name of the publisher:	Year:
(033)	Price	
	Other relevant information (Please write the tag and the corresponding data element).	
(044)	Vendor's Name and Address:	
	Type of Document	S/M/P/R/N/O

Note: With this minimum information, it is possible to create an order record and print an order letter. Afterwards, we can update the order record as and when necessary; once the book is received. we will have the complete information about the document. Then we can modify the order records to have a complete *accession record.*

Step B:

Key-in the data from the worksheet to a temporary file called In-Process file. This file contains the minimum required data elements to create an order file. Each record in the In-Process file consists of one data element and its tag. For example:

For Title:
033 $a Reproductive Health Management
For Author:
004 $a S.N. Deb

The last character in each of the order must be a special character, so that one can easily identify the end of the data elements. If the tag is 000, we may treat it as the end of a bibliographical record and if the tag is 999, we may treat it as the end of the file (in the In-Process file). Thus, the records in the In-Process file may look like:

	Record 1	....	Order information for document 1
	Record 2	....	document 1
	Record 3	....	
Block 1	Record 4	....	

	Record 5	....	
	Record 6	000........	
	Record 1	....	Order information for document 2
	Record 2	....	
	Record 3	....	
	Record 4	....	
	Record 5	000.......	
	Record 1	....	Order information for document
	Record 2	....	
Block n	Record 3	....	
	Record 4	....	
	Record 5	000.......	
Block(n+1)	Last Record 999	End of file	

Step C:

Processing the In-Process file to create an order file. For each block (consisting of information regarding order for a document) of information, we must create an order record, to be stored in the Order File. As and when the order is created an order letter (requesting for invoice or requesting for a book depending upon the situation) may be printed. After receiving the invoice, the order file may have to be processed again to print an order letter (requesting for a document); this letter may be sent to the vendor along with the cheque/draft, if necessary.

Step D:

Processing the Order file to

(i) send reminders;

(ii) send claim notices for replacement of defective copies; and

(iii) update the accession record in the accession file, etc.

Step E:

(i) Catalogue cards;

(ii) Book cards; and

(iii) Due date slips, etc.

Step F:

Processing the Order File and Fund File (once in a quarter or 6-9 months) to obtain financial statements and also to evaluate vendor performance, etc.

Programs to be Developed

A few programs required for the development of an automated acquisitions control system discussed below:

Program A:

To create an In-Process File. The required input may be on punched cards (tag + field indicator + data element) or straight away keyed-into the system (i.e. writing straight away on the floppy/disk/tape/cassette).

Program B:

To create an Order File and to print and order letter.

Program C:

To process an order file to send reminders, claim notices, etc.

Program D:

To update or search a record in the order file (That is to add a record or to search for a data element or a record in the order/file; and to add, or delete a data element within a record).

Program E:

To obtain various print-outs or lists from the Order File as and when necessary.

Program F:

To create an Accession File from the Order File.

Program G:

To process the Fund File to obtain various financial reports.

Programs D and E should be designed in such a way that one can even process the accession file using the same programs to update as well as to obtain various printed outputs.

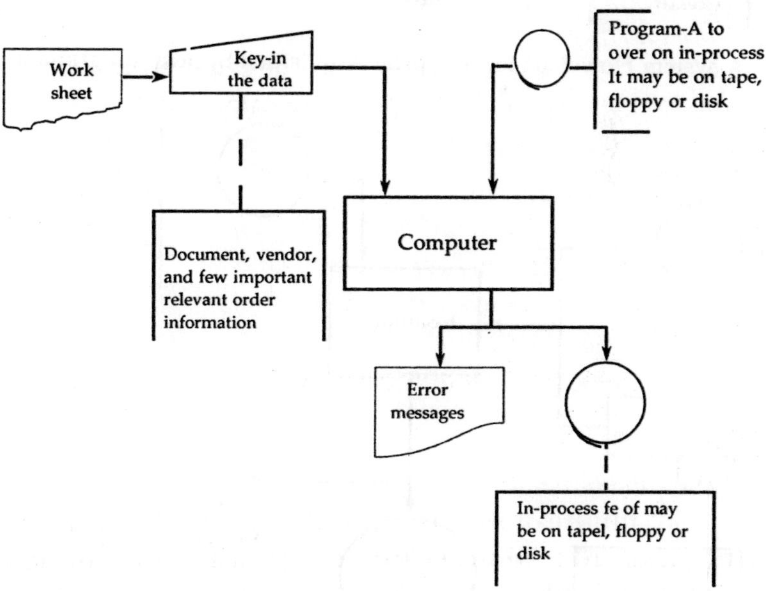

A System Flowchart for a Typical Acquisition System Program A.

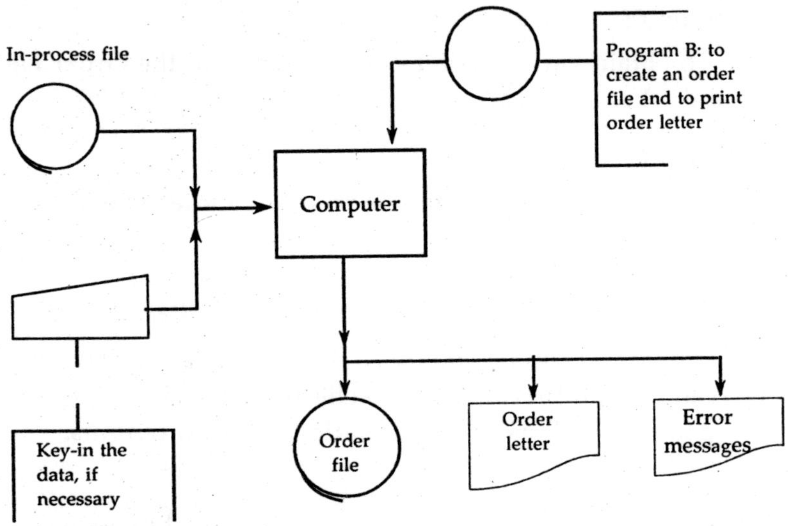

A system Flowchart for a Typical Acquisition System: Programme B.

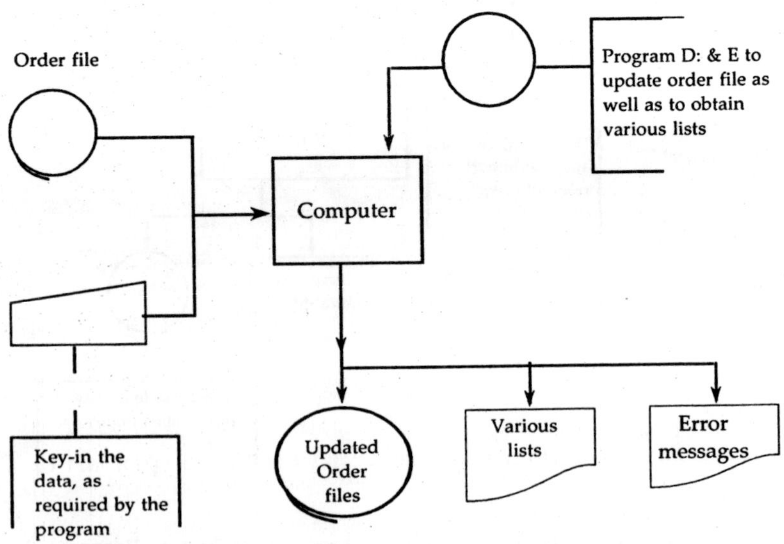

A System Flowchart for a Typical Acquisition System: Program D and E.

Serials Control

Automation of serials control system helps us to handle processing of serials more easily, quickly and economically. An automated serials control system is slightly different from that of a simple book ordering system. Because of the very nature of the serials, automated serials control systems are usually developed and designed independent of book ordering system. In contrast to books, serials are subscribed regularly. The cataloguing data (which are often changing) include additional information regarding the library's holding and it is to be regularly updated and also the information related to binding is to be processed regularly. An automated serials control system is expected to handle these procedures.

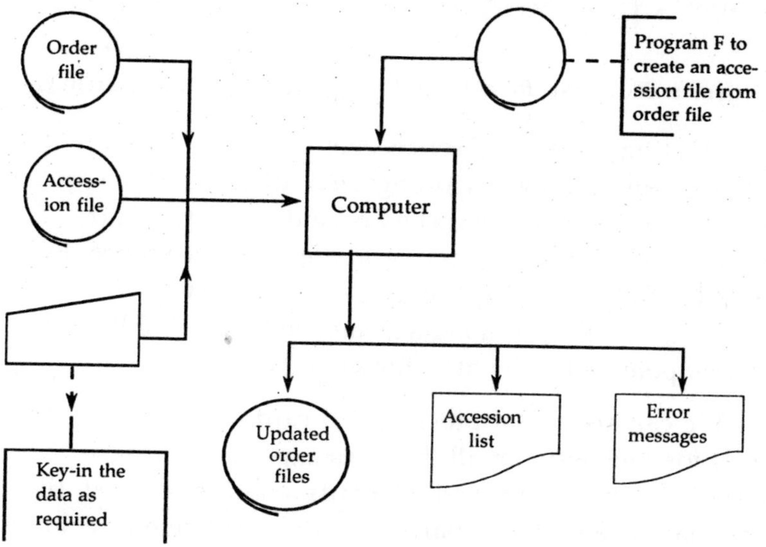

A System Flowchart for a Typical Acquisition System: program F.

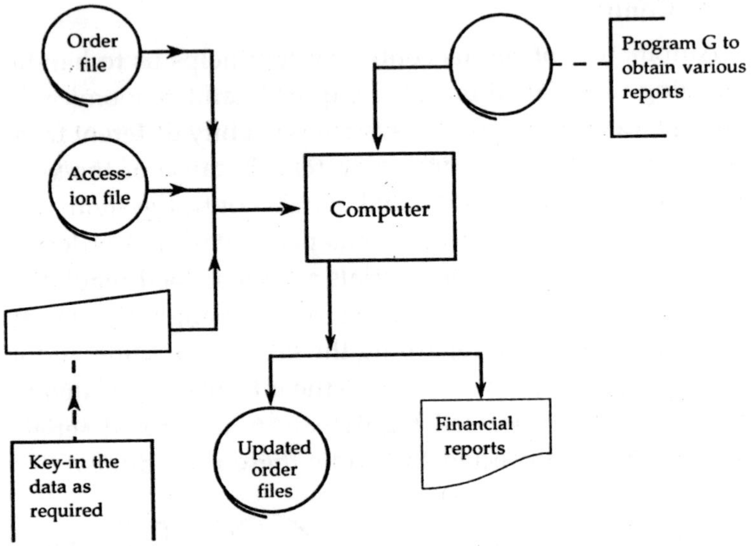

A System Flowchart for a Typical Acquisition System: Program G.

The simplest type of serials control system is the straight listing of information regarding each title. In such a system, the information is key punched or and then printed lists are obtained by title, by subject, or in any other sequence. Even in such a system, multiple copies of the library holdings can be produced easily and made available to users of library as well as potential users at remote points.

We can also use a pre-punched card (also called arrival card) for each issue of all the titles expected during a given period of time. The arrival cards contain a brief title, information about the particular issue expected (volume number, issue number, date and other information required in receiving process, frequency of publication etc.). The cards can be organised in a manual file. When issues are received, an attempt is made to match them against the corresponding arrival cards. These cards are pulled out and kept in a separate file. At the end of the month (assuming a monthly cycle of processing), the cards for the issues received are fed into the computer to update "holdings" information and it simultaneously punches another set of arrival cards for the next period. Any card remaining in the file at the end of a period represents issues which are potential claims.

Usually, there will not be any card-reader in a microcomputer system. So, if an automated serials control system is based on microcomputers, the arrival-file may be maintained on floppy disks and appropriately processed.

The Holding File of an automated serials control system can further be used to provide *holding data* (in machine-readable form) to those who want to compile union catalogue.

Functions of an Automated Serials Control System

General objectives of an automated serials control system are to handle serials and to maintain holding list.

In order to achieve these objectives, the system must perform the following functions:

1. Inputting serial data (those data which are essential to the system)
2. Ordering new serials
3. Renewals of presently subscribed serials
4. Cancellation of presently subscribed serials, if necessary
5. Accessioning of individual issues, as and when the issues are received
6. Sending reminders, if necessary
7. Claiming the issue, if necessary (such as, request for replacement of a defective copy)

8. Selective follow-up of missing issues
9. Preparation of various lists like:
   (a) List of periodicals received during a specified period;
   (b) List of periodicals cancelled during a specified period; and
   (c) List of holding with their status; on shelf, on binding, on circulation, etc. (the lists can be by subject, by country of origin, by title, etc.)
10. Keeping track of the amount spent on serials subscriptions, serials binding, etc. (subjectwise, if necessary)
11. Estimation of the budget for the next academic financial year
12. Binding Control.

These functions are not exhaustive; one can add many other functions, according to local needs.

Required Data Files

As has been discussed in the section on. "Acquisitions Control", several factors are to be considered while designing an automated serials control system. To perform the above mentioned functions, one may have to maintain at least the following files:

1. Order File
2. Holding File
3. Fund File

In a batch-processing system, these files may be maintained on magnetic tapes. For on-line system, it is necessary to maintain these files on disk.

In order to have as many data elements as possible in the order and the holding files, we can adopt a fixed cum variable field format similar to that of the MARC format.

Information in the fund file may be exactly similar to that described in the case of acquisitions control.

Data Elements in the Leader for Holding Record

Character Position	*Name of Description*	*Remarks*
0-4	Record Length	
5-9	Accession Number	
10	Mode of Acquisition	
11	Frequency of the Journal	
12	Type of Journal	
13	Foreign/Indian Publication	1=Indian 0=Foreign
14	Bound/Unbound volumes	B=Bound, U=Unbound
15	Complete/Incomplete	C=Complete I=Incomplete
16	Location in the library	
17-21	Base Address of the Data	
22-23	Used for local purposes	

Steps Involved in the Design and Development

In developing the system, the following steps are involved:

Step A:

Design a worksheet and fill the necessary information required for an order in it. The worksheet is given in the following table.

A Worksheet for Creating the In-Process File for Serials Control System

	Indian Statistical Institute Library *Bangalore-560059*	
(058)	Title of the serial	
(013)	Name of the publisher	
(014)	Place of publication	
(043)	Name and Address of vendor /Donor/Exchange	
(011)	Year of publication	
(008)	Volume number	Part/Issue
	Order for	
	New subscription /Renewal/Back-volume	
	Mode of Acquisition	E/S
	Frequency of the Journal	W/F/M/2/Q/4/H/Y/I
	Type of Journal	P/S/T/M
(001)	ISSN	(046) Order date

Issue No.	(033) Expected Arrival Date
X	XXXXXXX
X	XXXXXXX
X	1
1	1
1	1
X	XXXXXXX

Step B:

Key-in the data from the worksheet to a temporary file called In-Process file. This file contains order data. Each record in the In-Process file consists of one data element and its tag.

For example:

For title of a serial:

058 $a The Program#

For year:

011 SA1985#

For Expected Arrival Date

053 $a850731#

where # represents the field separate character.

Further, in the In-Process file, the records may be conveniently grouped and each group may be called as a block of information. A block may then be divided into two sub-blocks. The first sub-block for the minimum required data elements and the second sub-block for the issue numbers and their expected arrival dates. This is illustrated below:

1st sub-block consist of:	Order number, order date, order for a new subscription or for renewal, etc, mode of acquisition, frequency, type of journal ISSN, Year, Volume number, part number, title, name of the publisher, place of publication, name of the vendor and his/her address. (These data elements constitute a record in the block; price information may also be added at this stage, if available)
2nd sub-block consists of:	Issue numbers and the corresponding expected arrival dates; the data elements constitute a record in the block.

Step C:

Create an Order file. This means, processing the In-Process file to prepare order records. For each record (consisting of issue number and its expected arrival date) in the 2nd sub-block, an order record is created along with the information available in the 1st sub-block. That record is then written into the order file. If there are four issues for a given volume, four order records are created, one for each issue with its expected arrival date. As and when the block of information in the In-Process file is processed, an order letter (mainly requesting for invoice) is printed. After receiving the invoice, the order file may be processed along with the financial information, to print an order letter. This letter may be sent to the vendor along with the cheque/draft.

The steps involved in creating order records are given below:

1. Begin.
2. Read the first sub-block of the first block from the In-Process file.
3. Store the data elements appropriately in the memory allotted for the order record.
4. Read an issue No. and its expected arrival date from the second sub-block of the first block from the In-Process file.
5. Store them appropriately in the memory allotted for the order record.
6. Write the order record in the order file.
7. Create all the order records. (If there are 52 issues in a volume. 52 order records have to be created). Otherwise, repeat steps 4-6, until the records are created for each issue).
8. Process till all the blocks in the In-Process file are over and then stop. Otherwise go to step 2 to process next block.

Step D:

Processing the Order file, depending on the requirements for:

(a) sending reminders;

(b) sending claim notices; and

(c) preparing holding file, etc.

Step E:

Processing the Holding file to:–

(a) get catalogue cards, book cards, due date slips etc;

(b) complete and update the holding record; and

(c) get the binding statements.

Step F:

Processing Fund File as well as Order file to obtain financial statements.

Programs to be Developed

The following programs may have to be developed to have an automated serials control system.

Program A:

To create an In-Process file (This is exactly similar to that described in the case of acquisitions control).

Program B:

To create an Order file and simultaneously print an order letter.

Program C:

To process Order file (This may be similar to that described in the case of book acquisitions control) to:

(a) send reminder

(b) send claim notices

(c) create a holding record etc.

Program D:

To update a record in the Order File/holding File (to insert, delete and search a record; to insert/modify, delete and search a data element within a record). (This may be exactly similar to that described in the case of an acquisitions control).

Program E:

To obtain various print-outs or lists as and when necessary from the Order/Holding File.

Program F:

To process the fund file in order to obtain the necessary financial statements.

CIRCULATION CONTROL

Circulation, as a library function, is very specific definable and similar to common business activities such as material handling and inventory control. Circulation control is mainly concerned with the clerical function of keeping track of documents taken out of the library by the user i.e., of charging, discharging, overdue control, reserves, and associated file maintenance activities. It is therefore quite amenable for automation.

Several mechanised systems were developed for circulation control since World War I with considerable successes. A few them are Dickman's book charging system, Gaylord system, etc. The most popular and efficient mechanised circulation systems which were installed in some of the US libraries in the early 1930s used McBee punched cards. In this system, the McBee card was filled in with the author's name, title call number of the book, the user's name and address; the edge of the card is then punched, depending upon the date due.

The edge is thus clipped off over to the hole representing specific date on which that particular document is due. To find out books which are due on a particular date, a needle was inserted through the hole representing that date lifting all the McBee cards. Cards which refer to the relevant books that are due fall into a group thus effecting their retrieval. The cards were usually arranged by the call number. So, the librarian had access to the file of McBee cards neither by the date due or by the call number. In the 1950s a few librarians attempted to use computer generated lists and unit record equipment; the IBM-357 data collection terminal was the most popular unit record equipment which was used for automating circulation systems. In the late 1950s and 1960s, several libraries made use of the first and second generation computers respectively for automating their circulation systems. During this time batch processing systems were very popular. The rise of third generation computers in the early 1970s has made it possible for libraries to take advantage of on-line facilities for circulation systems in the mid 1970s.

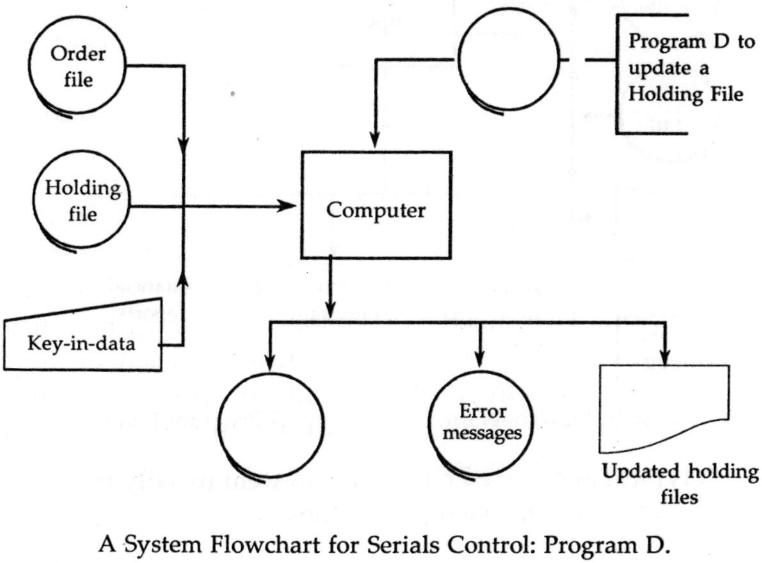

A System Flowchart for Serials Control: Program D.

Development in this field has thus taken place from systems based on unit record machines to batch processing systems and finally to a considerable number of partial on-line systems and then to real time on-line systems.

Functions of an Automated Circulation System

Automated circulation systems can be either traditional or broad in scope depending upon the design objectives established by the library. Thus, one of the basic considerations in the design and selection of a circulation system is the definition of the role and objectives of a circulation system in the library.

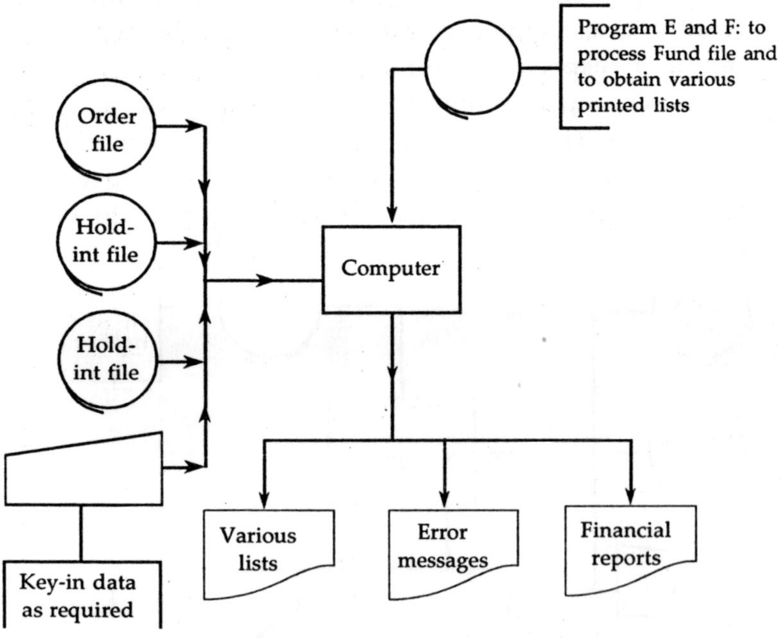

A System Flowchart for Serials Control Program E and F.

A typical automated circulation system usually performs some or all of the following functions:

1. Provision of information on the location of circulation items-either all the items or only those items on loan or elsewhere, i.e. at the bindery, on reserve, being recatalogued, etc.
2. Identification of items on loan to a particular borrower or class of borrowers (e.g., off-campus users).
3. Recording of *holds or personal reserves* for items on loan but desired by another borrower, often with additional provision for notifying the library staff when the item is returned and printing of *book available notice* to the requestor about the availability of the document.
4. Printing recall notices for items *on long-term loan,* when required by others.
5. Renewal of loans.
6. Notification to the library staff of overdue items and printing of overdue notices.
7. Notification to the library staff of delinquent borrowers (i.e., those with unpaid fines/or overdue books) either at the time of an attempted loan, or at the time a borrower is leaving the institution, or on request from the library.
8. Calculation of fines, printing of fine notices, recording receipt of fines, and sometimes printing details of fine receipts.
9. Calculation and printing various types of statistics.
10. Analysis of both summary statistics and statistics for the circulation of particular items for use in acquisitions, planning of services and for other administrative purposes.
11. Provision for handling special categories of borrowers and special types of materials.

12. Provision for printing *due date slips,* automatically generating orders for lost books or additional copies and printing mailing labels for remote borrowers.

These above functions are obviously in addition to the primary functions of the systems—charging and discharging of documents.

To achieve these objectives, circulation systems are designed to record and manipulate the following three kinds of information:

1. Information about the borrower (call number, identification number if it is other than the call number, author, title, date of publication, etc.).
2. Information about the document (call number, identification number if it is other than the call number, author, title, date of publication, etc).
3. Information about the transaction (such as date due or date of loan, and in some cases the time of loan).

Remarkably, these data are collected in a variety of ways. They way be entered by the borrower or by a library clerk and then keyed into the system. Alternatively, information on the borrower may be obtained automatically from a machine-readable identification card and information on the document borrowed may be automatically obtained from a previously punched book card placed in the book. In a micro system, information about both the users and documents may be displayed on the screens appropriately, by keying in the identification numbers. Then the relevant information may be re-written on a transaction file along with the transaction data. Information regarding the documents can be considered either as transitory (i.e., recorded in the transaction file when only an item is removed from its normal location) or as permanent systems (i.e., stored in the transaction file irrespective of where the book is). These two types of recording systems are respectively also known as Absence and Inventory systems. In the Former, the records are stored only during a document's absence from its normal location, and in the latter, the record is permanently stored in the file as long as the document is a part of the library's collection.

The data structure and the medium to store the necessary information may depend upon the above two systems. In an Absence System, the document record must contain enough information to identify the document. At least, it should consist of the call number, author and title. In an Inventory System, the document identification can consist of an arbitrary, but unique identifiction number. This number may then be used to link the more complete bibliographic data stored in the document file. In an Inventory System, the inventory file contains bibliographic records for all documents owned and therefore, the computer used by the library must have the capacity to process these records and to access them at a reasonable cost. On the other hand, an Absence System requires less file capacity and computer processing, and other things being equal, is less costly. Libraries with very large book collections may not find inventory systems economically feasible. In an Inventory Systems item information records are stored in a central file.

On the other hand, in an Absence System these are stored in the books themselves, generally in the form of a machine-readable punched card. Absence System, however, cannot provide information about documents that are not in circulation or have never been circulated. Because of the physical limitations in coding borrower's cards, all automated systems are of the inventory type when viewed from the perspective of the borrower file, i.e., a short, machine-readable identification code is assigned to each borrower and these codes are used to link the full records in a permanent borrower file.

Batch Versus Online Circulation Systems

Practically, Batch systems are usually dominated by the IBM-357 system. This machine accepts a punched card (end wise) in one slot and a plastic borrower's card punched with standard rectangular holes in another slot. For this system borrowers must, therefore, be issued with such cards and the books must have punched cards in them. When an identifiction card and a book card are placed in the device, the information from each is read automatically and transmitted by cable to an automatic card punch. The transaction date or due date is also transmitted at the same time. Returns are processed in a similar way, except that a special identification card is used to indicate that the transaction is a return and not a loan.

The transaction cards thus created on the remote punch for both charges and discharges contain all the required information on each transaction, and at the end of the day they are carried to a computer centre where they are used to update a magnetic tape file of all books in circulation. This updated file is printed out usually around mid-night and is made available the next morning for consultation by library staff and users (the list contains information such as the call number, borrower number, location of the book—if it is in reserve or at the bindery, *date due,* etc.)

At the same time, an updating run is made, overdues identified, notices printed and statistics compiled. But, in the recent past, many variations have been made on this basic pattern. Terminals other than the IBM-357 have been used; return transaction cards in some cases are produced while charging the book. The basic design of the system, however, remains the same.

The actual files are not directly accessible from the circulation desk in a batch processing system. The printed lists of the files are used instead. Depending on the size of the library, batch processing might take place daily or at any other convenient time interval. A certain portion of the files in the batch processing system is not accessible from the circulation desk until the next "batch" (job) is run. Reservation for certain books and identifying delinquent borrowers can be dealt in a batch system by *having a trapping-store device* in the data collection system. Without the trapping-store device, this can, however, be achieved only after the event, i.e., details of delinquent borrowers or list of reserved books would be printed out by the computer after processing the latest transaction record which may not be very effective. However, better results are obtained in an on-line system. The trapping-store system consists of an electronic store which is capable of holding document identification numbers.

It can trap books when they are returned. This can be done electronically by checking the book number of a return transaction against the numbers held in the store. If the number is present, an appropriate lamp glows which is an indication to the assistant at the library counter. Thus, the trapping-store device gives some automatic control over reservations even in a strictly batch or partially on-line system. If there is no such device, then a printed list of reserved items can be checked manually when the books are returned. On-line systems have certain advantages over the IBM-357 type or similar batch systems. In an on-line system, data are accessible at all times from the circulation desk upon enquiry. The status of the availability of each item is thus current at all times. On-line systems also elimiante the need for bulky print-outs.

Reservations for certain books (which are in circulation) in an online system can be dealt with immediately by recording the fact that an item is reserved by a particular user. The data related to the reservation is usually processed when the book is discharged or when the user is attempting to renew the book. Over-borrowing is solved simply by checking whether the borrower is within the allotted limits each time a book is issued. If a user tries to take out too many books, the computer can alert the library assistant at the circulation desk immediately about it. One of the problems faced by libraries wishing to operate on-line systems is the lack of available on-line facilities in the parent institution. Users normally take out and return books throughout the working hours of the library and to provide such a dedicated on-line system is beyond the capability of many institutions. To overcome this problem, a hybrid approach is often adopted. The main feature of such a system is the use of a library-in-house computer which offers some on-line facilities and a mainframe computer, usually belonging to the parent institution, for batch processing. The library-in-house computer may be a mini or a microcomputer. Some of the functions like charging, discharging, certain enquiries, reservation and detecting delinquent borrowers can be automated using the microcomputers.

Required Data Files

The above discussion relates to one basic choice of data structure whether the records in an automated circulation system should contain all library materials or only those which are in circulation. Another design choice is how these files will be accessed by the library processing? Relating the concepts of Absence or Inventory Systems to on-line or batch processing systems, we may thus see that there are basically four types of automated circulation systems:

1. On-line Absence Systems
2. On-line Inventory Systems
3. Batch processing Inventory Systems
4. Batch processing Absence Systems

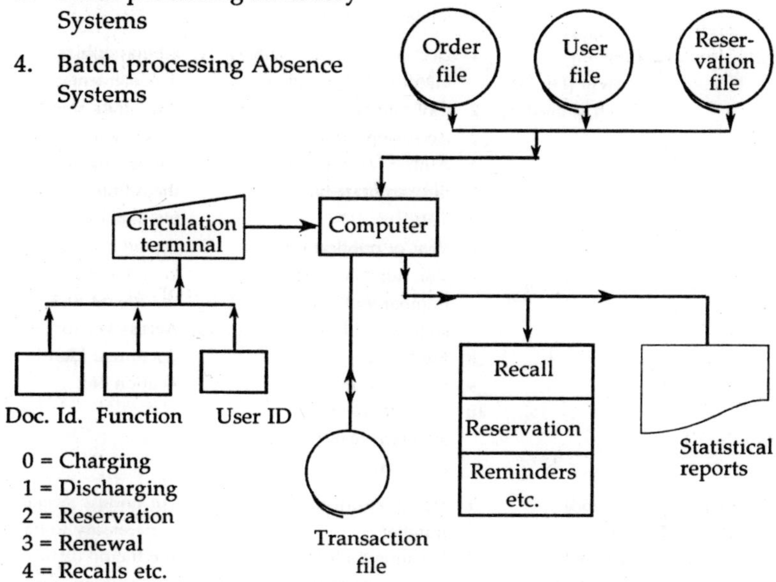

A System Flowchart for Circulation Control.

Data structures and media for storing the information may, therefore, depend upon a choice of one of the above four systems. Table 16.9 shows the files required with necessary data elements, access keys and the media to store the information for each of the above mentioned systems.

Data Elements for Circulation Files

S. No.	*File Name*	*System*	*Data Elements*	*Media*	*Remarks*
1	User File	For all the 4 systems	1 User identification Number 2 Name and address	Tape/ disk	For an on-line system, it is necessary to have the file on disk. Access key may be user

		3 Telephone number, if any, 4 Category (like students, faculty, etc.) 5 Subject interest		identification number
2 Document File	Inventory system (For both batch & on-line)	1 Document identification number 2 Call number 3 Accession number 4 Author (or name of the corporate body) 5 Title 6 Year of publication 7 Vol. number, part number and edition statement if any. 8 Publisher 9 Place of publication 10 Report/patent/ standard Nos. etc. if any	tape/ disk	1 Bibliographical data elements depending upon the type of documents. It is enough to store only the minimum possible data elements. 2 For on-line system, it is necessary to have the file on disk 3 Access key may be a document identification No.
3 Trans-action file	Absence (for both batch & on-line (systems)	1 User identification number 2 Document identification number (Call number of Accession number) 3 Author 4 Title 5 Year *Transaction Information* 6 Date of transaction or due date. 7 Kind of transaction (charging. discharging etc.,) 8 Location of the transaction (whether it is in branch library etc.)	Tape/ disk	1 For on-line system, it is necessary to have the file on disk. It is enough store only the minimum possible data elements (who borrowed when and what etc.) 2 Access key may be a document identification number or a user identification number or both.
4 Trans-action	Inventory (for both batch	1 User identification number		

file	and on-line systems)	2 Document identification number 3 Item numbers 6, 7 and 8 of the Absence Transaction file (transaction information)		
5 Delinquent Borrowere file	On-line (for both Inventory and Absence)	(Same as USer file)		Instead of maintaining a separate file, we can have an additional data element pertaining to delinquency (0=delinquent borrower; otherwise 1) in the user file.
6 Delinquent Borrowers'	Batch processing (For both Inventory & Absence)	1 User number identification 2 Status. (type of delinquency)	Tape	
7 Request file	For all the 4 systems	1 User identification number 2 Document identification number 3 Data, when the book is reserved.,	Tape/ disk/ cassette/ floppy	If the system is on-line, it is better to store on CD or floppy or a cassette.

Methods of Inputting Identification Numbers

The simplicity of an automated circulation system depends upon how best we can record both the document and user identification numbers at the circulation desk at the time of charging/discharing a document. There are several ways of recording the identification numbers. Some of these are:

Document Identification Number

In an automated circulation systems, each document usually carries a punched card with some minimum required information for identifying the document. the minimum required data for a document are:

Document Identification Number (=DIN) (12 characters)
Authors (15 characters)
Title (25 characters)
Edition number, if any (2 characters)
Volume number, if any (2 characters)
Year of publication (4 characters)
Name of publisher (10 characters)
Place of publisher (10 characters)

The crux of the problem here is what should be the DIN? It can be any one of the following:

(a) Call number
(b) Accession number
(c) Serial number (which is different from accession number)
(d) ISBN
(e) Any other code such as author-title code.

The choice of DIN depends upon the hardware device used to record the DIN. For example, if one uses a light pen device to record DIN, one can even use coded labels as DIN such as a bar-coded label consisting of a few white and black bars of varied thickness. The bar codes can be affixed to the spine or inside back cover of the document. The choice of DIN further depends upon whether it is Absence or Inventory system. The DIN, in an Inventory System, can be brief since a record for each document in the collection is stored with complete information in a machine-readable inventory file.

User Identification Number

A user identification number (UIN) can be punched on a plastic card, if a suitable hardware device is available. it can even be punched on punched cards. But, in this case, the punched cards should be stored at the circulation desk which not only requires sufficient space, but pose some difficulties to retrieve at the time of charging and discharging a document. One can also give this through a keyboard in which case, UIN is typed for each transaction. It can be any one of the following:

(a) Roll numbers or Registered numbers assigned by the library or parent organisation

(b) Social security or insurance number, if any

(c) Name

Design Factors

The above discussion leads to consider the following factors in designing a circulation system:

(a) choice of system (whether Absence/Inventory System)

(b) Mode of operation (batch/on-line processing)

(c) Method of inputting identification numbers

(d) Available hardware.

As such one can obtain a variety of statistics from the automated circulation control, after at no additional cost. These statistics can, in turn, be used for decision-making purposes for future.

4

Classification in Practice

"Whenever you argue with another wiser than yourself in order to that others may admire your wisdom, they will discover your ignorance."

—**Saadi**

Most traditionally, the following seven are the widely known modern schemes of classification:

Name of scheme	*Contracted name*
Decimal Classification	DC
Expensive Classification	BC
Universal Decimal Classification	UDC
Congress Classification	LC
Subject Classification	SC
Colon Classification	CC
Bibliographic Classification	BC

"Of all these", it has been said, "two are more or less obsolete (Brown and Cutter), two are moribund but might be revived by blood transfusion of new thinking (Dewey and UDC)". The same source speaks of the Colon Classification as "the best of the published schemes, exemplifying the most original and the most creative thinking in the field". Having discussed the essential qualities of an efficient scheme of classification, Palmer and Wells say, "We find that the only scheme produced so far which comes within measurable distance of this ideal is the Colon Classification", The later chapters of this part give extracts, suited to small public libraries, from CC as well as DC. Therefore, a more detailed evaluation of these two schemes is given below. The relative schedules in the later chapters can form the basis for comparison of helpfulness of sequence.

Colon Classification

Valid Principles

According to Bliss, "The system is constructed on valid principles .. . the 'basic' classification is logical in most of its divisions, scientific in details, and scholarly in its elaboration". Its basis is utterly different from that of the Decimal Classification. It is based on the Meccano principle. Hence its hospitality is virtually unending. Indeed', it is a self-perpetuating scheme of classification.

Synthetic and Mnemonic

According to Phillips, "The objects sought through this synthetic method are minuteness of classification — extending to the individualising of every book in the library — a high mnemonic value, hospitality, and elasticity, combined with great brevity as to the printed schedules... the process of subdividing by topic is normally simple, and figures are used decimally, but there are many divisions where a succession of characteristics is applied in order".

Provision for Indian Subjects

CC is universal in its scope. Without prejudice to this, it gives detailed schedules for the geographical divisions, languages, religions, and philosophical systems of India. It has a simple method of classifying literature. In this method, the literature in any language of the world, including those of India, can be readily classified by a classifier. This is typical of the autonomy given by CC to the classifier.

Provision for Indian Classics

India is rich in ancient classics. These classics are being continuously brought out in new editions and translations. They are popular. Most of the public libraries in India acquire them. They are much in demand. CC gives a fairly exhaustive schedule of the Indian classics in Medicine, Spiritual Experience, Fine Arts, Literary Criticism, Linguistics, Religion, and Philosophy. The schedule was constructed with the help of my friend Mahamahopadhyaya Professor S Kuppuswamy Sastri, an authority on Indian Classics. According to Sayers, "It has an admirable scheme for arranging the Indian literatures, the fullest I know". This schedule of Indian classics forms Part 3 of CC. It is in 136 pages. It is not, therefore, practicable to reproduce that schedule in this small book. The original book itself must be used.

Provision for Depth Classification

It has now been discovered that a set of postulates had been guiding the building up of CC from the unconscious levels. They have now been brought to the conscious level. This makes it possible to fit CC to any involved depth of classification needed for the documentation service of specialist readers. In other words, the hospitality of CC is very rich. As a result, without in any way lengthening the class numbers of the books normally kept in public libraries for the general public, CC gives expressive, individualising, and therefore necessarily long numbers to the articles found in learned periodicals. The continuation of the same system of classification from ordinary books to articles in periodicals is an advantage to readers.

This helpful result has not been achieved by any other scheme. On account of this, there is often talk about the need for special schemes of classification for special subjects for learned readers. But this capacity of CC is used by some librarians, in an irresponsible way without actual experience in classification, to make a glib statement like, "Oh ! CC is quite learned, I grant. It can be used for documentation, it is obvious. But it is too complicated for use in public or school libraries." This erroneous impression is due to the ignorance of the quite simple class numbers given by CC for subjects which are usually represented by the books in a public library. These subjects are of a general kind and not of a specialised nature.

Short Class Number

The CC numbers are not only simple-looking, but are also comfortably short for books normally found in public libraries. Here again, by simply looking at the numbers arising in the depth classification needed in documentation work, people without experience make the irresponsible statement that CC number is long. The correct way of deciding the relative length of different systems of class numbers is the statistical way. To pursue this way, one should take a random sample of a large number of individualising class numbers of the same subjects, got by different schemes. Their average lengths should be compared. A comparative statistical study of CC and DC class numbers in this manner has been done. According to the results of this study, on an average, a CC number has one digit less than a DC number.

Marathi and Hindi Versions

A Marathi version of CC has been brought out by R S Parkhi. This must be of use to Maharashtra librarians not knowing English. A Hindi version of extracts has also been published. As a result of the current Indian renascence, versions in the other modern Indian languages may be brought out in due course.

Decimal Classification

Inadaptability

According to Bliss, "The Decimal Classification is disqualified ... both structurally and functionally. It does not embody the natural, scientific, logical and educational orders. It fails to apply consistently the fundamental principles of classification .... It is inefficient in classifying the modern literature for specific topics.... Nor is its vogue among librarians and even among scientists and businessmen especially significant, except for the fact that there was nothing else readily available. It is an antiquated and inadaptable product .... And now it is hopelessly beyond reconstruction". According to Schofield, "owing to lack of adaptation to changed conditions 'Dewey' is out of touch with modern knowledge, it has also lost contact with the stock and demand of the libraries which use it".

Poor Hospitality

DC can give a class number to Agriculture of Rice Plant; and it can also give a class number to Manuring in Agriculture; but it cannot give a class number for Manuring of Rice Plant. Similarly, there is a DC Number for the Medicine of the Bone system; and there is also a DC number for Tuberculosis; but there is no DC number for Tuberculosis of the Bone. Again, Elementary Education has a DC number; and Curriculum has a DC number; but there is no DC number for Curriculum for Elementary Education. On the other hand, CC can furnish a number for all these combinations and even for more complicated combinations such as Time for Applying Cow Dung Manure to Rice Plant in Monsoon Areas of India.

No Provision for Indian Subjects

DC is far too American in its schedules. It has no satisfactory schedules for the geographical divisions, languages, literature, religions, and philosophical systems of India. It has no device at all to bring a classic and its family of books together. Dewey read in the *Five Laws of Library Science* (1931) about CC being designed. Thereupon, he wrote to me saying that DC was poor in Indian subjects and that he would welcome our collaboration in removing this defect in DC. But unfortunately, he died before the CC came out in print – indeed shortly after he wrote to me.

Recommendation

CC is a later invention than DC. DC has all honour for its pioneership in making classification popular. But it has also the handicaps of a pioneer. It has been outmoded. Its structure is based on a constricted foundation. Its notation is not sufficiently mnemonic. Its hospitality has been outgrown by the march of knowledge. Having witnessed all such natural defects in the pioneer DC, CC has based its structure on a very elastic foundation, almost reaching the bed-rock of the seminal level. It has great hospitality and mnemonics. It has developed certain devices to withstand the challenge of the turbulent and ever-growing universe of knowledge. Its versatility has been described to be such that every new subject creates its own class number in the scheme. The British Classification Group has therefore accepted that, "Facet Analysis (the technique of CC) must be the basis of a classification scheme able to meet requirements". On these grounds, CC is recommended for adoption. In Indian libraries, there should be the additional secondary reason of its being of Indian origin.

Classifying

Class Number

The Class Number of a book is a translation of the name of its specific subject into the artificial language of ordinal numbers specified and elaborated by a scheme of classification.

Examples

CC	*Subject*	*DC*
J	Agriculture	63
J1	Horticulture	63
J16	Floriculture	635
J169	Bulb plants	635.944
J16912	Tulip	635.93114
J16912:2	Manure for tulip	
116912:2:3	Application of manure to tulip	
116912:2:3.245	Application of manure to tulip in Nepal	

Ultimate Class

The Ultimate Class of a book is the class of the smallest extension, admitted by the scheme of classification into which it can be placed.

Book Number

The purpose of Book Number is to individualise the different books having the same ultimate class. In CC the book number is a translation of the names of certain specified features of the book into an artificial language of ordinal numbers specified and elaborated by rules. In DC, it may be made of the first three letters of the name of the author.

Call Number

Call number = Class number + Book Number + indication of any abnormal peculiarity of a book such as being a pamphlet or an organised some etc, if any. A double space should separate the class number and the book number.

Examples

CC	*Subject*	*DC*
J16 N59	Sarada (L). Floriculture. 1959 (in English, which is taken to be the Favoured language of the library)	635 Sar
J16 152N59	(If the book is in Hindi)	635 Sar
JI6 c5N59	(If the book is an alphabetical list in English)	635 Sar
J16 152c5N59	(If the book is an alphabetical list in Hindi)	635 Sar
J16 N59	(If the first of the above books is a pamphlet)	635 Sar

The inability of DC to provide distinguishing call numbers for the five different kinds of books on floriculture can be easily seen.

The Book Number is written below the Class Number on the spine of the book and on the back of the title-page of the book.

Examples

JI6	JI6	J16	635
N59	152N59	c5N59	Sar

Classifying

Classifying is constructing the Class Number and the Book Number of a book, according to the Classification Scheme used. If the book is abnormal, in any way, that too should be indicated. Classificationist designs a scheme of classification. Classifier uses the scheme and classifies books.

SCHEDULE OF MAIN CLASSES

CC	*Name of Class*	DC
	Generalia	
a	Bibliography	01
k	Cyclopaedia	03
m	Periodical	05
n	Serial	058
P	Conference proceedings	063
w	Biography	92
z	Collection	08
	Specific and Partially Comprehensive	
1	Universe of knowledge	
2	Library science	02
3	Book science	
4	Journalism	07
A	Science (general)	5
B	Mathematics	51
C	Physics	53
D	Engineering	62
E	Chemistry	54
F	Technology	66
G	Biology	57
H	Geology	55,56
HZ	Mining	
I	Botany	58
J	Agriculture	63
JB	Forestry	634.9
K	Zoology	59
KZ	Animal husbandry	636 to 639
L	Medicine	61
M	Useful arts	6
D	Spiritual experience	149.3

N	Fine arts	7
∝	Humanities	
O	Literature	8
P	Linguistics	4
Q	Religion	2
R	Philosophy	1
S	Psychology	15
S	Social sciences	3
T	Education	37
U	Geography	91
V	History	9
W	Political Science	32
X	Economics	33, 38, 65
Y	Sociology	31,36,39
YZ	Social work	
Z	Law	34

SCHEDULES OF COMMON ISOLATES

Anteriorising Common Isolates

CC	*Isolates*	*DC*
a	Bibliography	
c	Concordance	
.d	Table	
e	Formula	
f	Atlas	
k	Cyclopaedia	03
m	Periodical	04 if organ of a body and otherwise,
n	Serial	05 06
p	Conference proceedings	
v	History	

w	Biography	
x	Works (Collection or Selection)	09
y1	Programme of instruction	
y2	Syllabus	
y3	Synopsis	
y4	Scope	
y7	Case study	
y8	Digest	

Meaning of Common Isolate

The significance of the term "Common Isolate" is that it can be added to any subject. The following examples illustrate this significance.

CC	*Subject with Cummon Isolate*	*DC*
Ik	Cyclopaedia of agriculture	630.3
J:4k	Cyclopaedia of plant disease	632.03
J16k	Cyclopaedia of floriculture	635.03
J16912k	Cyclopaedia of tulip	635.9311403
J16912:4k	Cyclopaedia of diseases of tulip	
J16912:4:5k	Cyclopaedia of prevention of diseases of tulip	

Significance of "Anteriorising"

The significance of the term "Anteriorising Isolate" is that the subject formed by attaching it to a host subject comes earlier than the host subject.

1	*Jk*	Cyclopaedia of agriculture (comes earlier than)
	J	Agriculture.
2	*b,m*	Periodical in medicine (comes earlier than)
	L	Medicine.
3	Tv	History of education (comes earlier than)
	T	Education.

In DC, all common isolates are only posteriorising.

Facets for Anteriorising Common Isolates

Some of the anteriorising common isolates may have to be divided further by the addition of a geographical number and/or a chronological number. These two numbers are to be separated by a dot as specified or a comma. Adding a Geographical Number is called Geographical Device (=GD). Adding a Chronological Number is called Chronological Device(=CD). The following is the table of facets for anteriorising common isolates.

Common Isolate		*Facet by (GD)*	*Facet by (CD)*
k		Geographical area of purview	Epoch of origin worked out to the minimum number of digits necessary for individualisation
m	Periodical	Country of origin, or country of sponsoring body, if organ of a body	do
n	Serial	Geographical area of purview	do
p	Conference (periodical)	do	do
p	Conference (isolated)	do	Year of the conference
v	History	do	Latest effective epoch covered
w	Biography (collective)		Latest effective decade among the years of birth of the biographees
w	Biography (single)		Year of birth of the biographee
x	Works (collective)		Latest effective decade among the years of birth of the authors included
x	Works (single)		Year of birth of the author

Note: Latest effective decade is a decade whose decade number ends with 1 or 3, or 5, or 7, or 9, as explained in the section "Last Effective Decade".

Examples

CC	*Category*	*DC*
*k*3,*L*	Encyclopaedia Brittanica (which has a slant to Great Britain and which was started in 1768)	03
*k*73,N	Encyclopaedia Americana (started in 1903)	03
*k*73,N3	Columbia Encyclopaedia (started by Columbia University, USA, in 1935)	03
Am2,N	Transactions, Bose Research Institute (started in India in 1917)	504
Am2,Nl	Journal, Indian Institute of Science (started in India in 1918)	504
Am2,N3	Current Science (started in India in 1932)	505
Am2,N34	Proceedings, sec A, Indian Academy of Sciences (started in 1934)	504
Aw3,M	Transactions, Cambridge Philosophical Society (started in 1818)	504
Am3,M6	Nature (started in Great Britain in 1869)	505
Bv2.F5	History of Indian mathematics up to 1150's	510.954
By2.N3	History of Indian mathematics up to 1930's	510.954
BwK42	Biography of Newton	925.1
BwM88	Biography of Ramanujan	925.1

Note 1. DC mixes up all cyclopaedias on a subject alphabetically, whatever be the country of slant. But CC individualises each cyclopaedia — that is, no two cyclopaedias have the same CC number. As a result, the cyclopaedias in a subject get separated out by the countries of slant; and those with slant to the same country get arranged by their years of origin.

2. DC separates out independent periodicals from those sponsored by a learned body or an institution. But CC does not do so.
3. DC mixes up all periodicals in a subject alphabetically whatever be the country or year of origin or language. But CC individualises each periodical — that is, no two periodicals have the same CC number. As a result, the periodicals in a subject get separated out and grouped by countries of origin; and those of the same country get arranged by their years of origin.
4. DC cannot indicate the period up to which the history of a subject is brought. But CC indicates it. As a result, the histories of a subject get arranged by periods.
5. DC cannot separate out the biographies of different persons in a subject. But CC individualises the biographies of each person — that is, the biographies of no two persons have the same CC number. As a result, the biographies of different persons in the same subject get arranged by the years of birth of the biographees.

Anteriorising Common Isolates Applicable Only After Space Facet

CC	*Isolate*	*DC*
r	Administration report Statistics (if periodical)	

Examples

1. CC number for ad initiation report on Indian education is

T.2r and not Tr2

2. CC number for the periodical of Indian medical statistics started in 1902 is

L.2sN and not Ls2,N

Anteriorising Common Isolate Applicable Only After Time Facet

CC	*Isolate*	DC
s	Statistics (if stray)	
t	Commission report	
t4	Survey	
t5	Plan	
t7	Ideal	
v	Sources of history	
v5	Literature	
v6	Tradition	
v7	Archaeology etc	
v8	Archives	

Examples

CC	*Category*	DC
T4.2.Nt	Report of the Indian University Commission of 1917	
T4.2.N4t	Report of the Indian University Commission of 1948	
T4.3.Nt	Report of the British University Commission of 1908	

Posteriorising Personality Common Isolate

CC	*Personality Isolate*	DC
d	Institution	
f	Investigating institution	
f2	Observational	
f3	Experimenting	
f4	Discussional	

f7	Yogic (Asrama)
g	Learned institution
t	Educational institution
t2	Lower
t4	Higher (To be divided as in T)
y	Profession

*Note:*1. A comma is to precede a posteriorising personality common isolate.

2. To individualise an institution, the common isolate number is to be followed successively by a comma, the number of its country, and the first letter of the name of its locality. If a second locality has such an institution, the first two letters (both in capitals) of its name are to be added. And so on.

Examples

CC	*Institution*	*DC*
B9,t2,3G	Royal Observatory (Greenwich)	
D,f41,2B	Engineering College (Bombay)	
D,t41,2BA	Engineering College (Bangalore)	
D,t41,2BAR	Engineering College (Baroda)	
E.t3,2P	National Chemical Laboratory (Poona)	

Posteriorising Energy Common Isolates

CC	*Energy Isolate*	*DC*
f	Investigation	
f2	Observation	
f3	Experiment	
g	Criticism	

Note. A colon is to precede an energy common isolate.

Examples

CC	Subject	DC
2:51N3:g	Criticism of Colon Classification	
B96:f2	Observation of stars	
C:f3	Practical physics	
C6:f3	Practical electricity	
O15:g	Criticism of Sanskrit literature	
T15:3:f2	Observation of elementary school teaching	

Time Isolates

CC	Time Isolate	CC	Time Isolate
A	Before 9999 BC	L	1700 to 1799 AD
Al	Eozoic	M	1800 to 1899 AD
A2	Palaeozoic	N	1900 to 1999 AD
A3	Mesozoic	P	2000 to 2099 AD
A4	Cainozoic	Q	2100 to 2199 AD
A5	Quartenary	R	2200 to 2299 AD
B	9999 to 1000 BC	S	2300 to 2399 AD
C	999 to 1 BC	T	2400 to 2499 AD
D	1 to 999 AD	U	2500 to 2599 AD
E	1000 to 1099 AD	V	2600 to 2699 AD
F	1100 to 1199 AD	w	2700 to 2799 AD
G	1200 to 1299 AD	X	2800 to 2899 AD
H	1300 to 1399 AD	YA	2900 to 2999 AD
I	1400 to 1499 AD		
J	1500 to 1599 AD		
K	1600 to 1699 AD		

Note. DC has no schedule of time isolates for general use as common isolates.

Use of Time Isolates

Time forms a posteriorising common isolate. It has to be added at the end of a subject for all historical accounts and local descriptions of it. Sometimes an isolate is formed, or sharpened — that is, subdivided — by the addition of time isolate. This is called Chronological Device (CD).

Construction of Time Isolates for Modern Period

1. For a decade, add the decade digit after the century digit.
2. For a year, add the year digit after the decade digit.

Construction of Time Isolate for Mediaeval Period

1. For a century, add the century digit after the millennium digit D.
2. For a decade, add the decade digit after the century digit.
3. For a year, add the year digit after the decade digit.

Last Effective Decade

The number of a Last Effective Decade will end with I when the Natural Decade Number ends with 0 or 1; with 3 when the natural decade number ends with 2 or 3; with 5 when the natural decade number ends with 4 or 5; with 7 when the natural decade number ends with 6 or 7, and with 9, when the natural decade number ends with 8 or 9.

Explanation

Experience has shown that grouping by intervals for about one generation is more helpful and also sufficient in the arrangement of books on shelves. It also makes the work of the classifier less arduous. This is perhaps because a generation is a more natural and significant unit in the progress of human thought and practices than a decade which is only arbitrary and arithmetical. Generally, in history and local description, the Last Effective Decade is to be used.

Space Isolates, That is Geographical Divisions

CC	*Area*	*DC*
1	World	
1-0	Empire to be divided by (GD) *(Illustrative)*	
1-52	Roman empire	
1-56	British empire	
16	Atlantic countries	
161	Mediterranean countries	
167	Baltic countries	
17	Pacific countries	
19	By Zone	
191	Equatorial	
192	Tropical	
1923	South	
1927	North	
193	Sub-tropical	
195	Temperate	
197	Sub-arctic	
198	Arctic	
19A	By Orientation	
19B	East	
19C	Near East	956
19D	Middle East	956
19E	Far East	
19F	South-East	959
19G	South	
19L	South-West	

19M	West	
19R	North-West	
19S	North	
19W	North-East	
19X	Inside	
19Y	Outside	
1A	Near-Sovereign Formation	
To be divided by (CD) *(Illustrative)*		
IN	League of Nations area	
1N4	United Nations area	
1N48	The Commonwealth area	
Division by (SD) *(Illustrative)*		
1(P111)	English speaking countries	
1(Q7)	Muslim countries	
1(Y:42)	Under-developed countries	
2	Mother country (India)	54
21	Southern States	548
211	Madras (Tamil Nadu)	548.2
212	Kerala	548.3
213	Mysore (Karnataka)	548.7
216	Andhra Pradesh	
23	**Western States**	544
231	Bombay	547.9
235	Maharashtra	
236	Gujarat	
237	Rajasthan	543.42
24	North Western States	
241	Delhi	545.6
243	Punjab (East)	545.5
245	Himachal Pradesh	545.2
247	Jammu and Kashmir	546

25	**Northern States**	542
252	Uttar Pradesh	542.5
255	Madhya Pradesh	543.3
27	**Eastern States**	
271	Orissa	541.3
273	Bihar	541.2
275	Bengal (West)	541.4
277	Assam	541.6
28	**Centrally administered areas**	
297	Himalayan States	
297	Bhutan	541.9
2973	Sikkim	542.7
2975	Nepal	542.6
3	**Favoured country (Great Britain)**	
31	England	42
32	Wales	429
33	Scotland	41
34	Ireland	415
4	**Asia**	**5**
41	China	51
42	Japan	52
43	South-east Asia	59
431	Indo-China	597
433	Thailand	593
435	Malay States	595
436	Indonesia	991
438	Burma	591
4498	Ceylon	548.9
44Q7	Pakistan	547
44Q71	East Pakistan	
44Q72	East Bengal	541.45
44Q73	West Pakistan	
44Q74	Sind	547.3

44Q75	Baluchistan	588
44Q77	West Punjab	545.3
45	Persia (Iran)	55
46	Arabian Peninsula	53
461	Arabia	538
465	Palestine	
4651	Jordan	569.5
4653	Israel	569.4
4655	Lebanon	569.2
466	Syria	569.1
467	Iraq (Mesopotamia)	567
4671	Babylonia	
4672	Assyria	
47	Asia Minor	
48	Siberia	57
4893	Armenia	
49	Other Asian countries	
491	Afghanistan	581
494	Manchuria	518
495	Korea	519
496	Mongolia	517
497	Sinkiang	516
498	Tibet	515
5	**Europe**	**4**
51	Greece	495
52	Italy	45
5291	Sicily	458
5222	Malta	458.2
53	France	44
54	Spain and Portugal	
541	Spain	46
542	Portugal	469

55	Germany	43
5541	Saar Basin	
57	Scandinavia	48
571	Sweden	485
572	Denmark	489
573	Norway	481
574	Iceland	491
575	Finland	471
58	Russia	47
591	Turkey	496
59191	Cyprus	564
592	Balkan States	496
5931	Austria	436
5932	Hungary	4391
594	Switzerland	404
595	Poland	438
596	Netherlands	492
5961	Belgium	493
5962	Holland	492
5971	Lithuania	
5973	Latvia	474
5975	Esthonia	474
6	**Africa**	**6**
63	Union of South Africa	68
671	Egypt	62
682	Abyssinia	63
7	**America**	**7**
71	North America	7
7191	Greenland	98
72	Canada	71
73	United States	73
74	Mexico	72

7414	Yucatan	726
75	Central America	728
791	South America	3
792	West Indies	739.13
8	**Australia**	**94**
937	New Zealand	993
	Oceans	
95	Indian Ocean	
96	Atlantic Ocean	997
97	Pacific Ocean	99
983	Antarctic Ocean	
987	Artic Ocean	98

Note

1. For more detailed divisions, schedule 4 of CC should be used.
2. Orientation divisions and subject divisions of any geographical area can be got on the analogy of the respective divisions of "1 World".
3. There are no appropriate DC numbers for certain geographical divisions.

Use of Space Isolates

Space forms a posteriorising common isolate. It has to be added at the end of the class number of any subject, for all its historical and descriptive accounts. Sometimes, an isolate is formed or sharpened — that is, subdivided — by the addition of space isolate. This is called Geographical Device (GD).

Examples

1. Individualisation of cyclopaedias and periodicals.
2. The first facet in the main class "V History".
3. The first facet in the main class "Z Law".

Physiographical Isolates

CC	*Physiographical Isolate*	DC
1	Land	
121	Desert	
124	Forest	
131	Coastland	
133	Cape	
137	Delta	
14	Island	
16	Valley	
2	Mountain	
3	City (Town, Village)	
535	Inland sea	
54	Lake	
6	River	

Note:1. There is no provision in DC for physiographical isolates.

2. In CC the isolate number of a physiographical isolate should be added to the host space isolate of the least area containing it.
3. A dot should separate the host isolate number and the physiographical isolate number.
4. A particular physiographical entity may be got by alphabetical device, as shown in some of the following examples

Examples

CC	*Physiographical Feature*	DC
2.121	Indian deserts	
2.121R	Rajputana desert	
2.6	Indian rivers	
2.6G	Ganges	

21.6	South Indian rivers
21 .6K	Kavery
211.3	Cities of Madras State
211.3T	Tanjore
211.3T1	Tirunelveli
73.3N	New York (City)

Parts of Physical Features (Illustrative)

CC	*Parts of Physical Features*	*DC*
2.6G.1	Sources of the Ganges	
4.2H	Himalayas	
4.2H.1	Peaks of Himalayas	
4.2H.1E	Mount Everest	
5.2A.1B	Mount Blanc	

Examples

CC	*Subject*	*DC*
U8.2.6G.1	Journey to the source of the Ganges	
US.4.2H	Himalayan travels	
U8A2H.1E	Mount Everest expedition	

Language Isolates

CC	*Language*	*DC*
1	Indo-European	
11	Teutonic	
111	English	2
113	German	3
12	Latin	7
122	French	4
124	Portuguese	69
13	Greek	8

15	Sanskrit	912
151	Prakrit	913
1511	Pali	913.791
1512	Maharastri	
1516	Ardhamagadhi	
1517	Magadhi	
1518	Apabhramsa	
15198	Sinhalese	914.8
1521	Hindi	914.3
153	Punjabi	914.2
154	Gujarati	914.7
155	Marathi	914.6
156	Oriya	914.5
157	Bengali	915.4
158	Nepali	
16	Iranian	915.5
164	Persian	915.5
168	Urdu	914.3
2	Semitio	92.8
25	Hebrew	92.4
28	Arabic	92.7
3	Dravidian	948.1
31	Tamil	948.11
32	Malayalam	948.12
33	Kanarese	948.14
34	Tulu	948.15
35	Telugu	948.13
36	Kui	
38	Brahui	
39	Toda etc	
41	Chinese	95.1
42	Japanese	956
433	Siamese	959.1

435	Malay	992.21
438	Burmese	958
99M87	Esperanto	089.2

Uses of Language Isolates

Language is a common isolate. It forms the first facet in the main classes "O Literature" and "P Linguistics". In each of these cases it is a personality facet. Language forms a facet in book numbers also.

SCHEDULE OF SELECT CLASS NUMBERS

This chapter gives a schedule of Class Numbers for books likely to be found in a small public library. These Class Numbers are ready-made ones for the convenience of use by a semi-professional. They are illustrative only. Similar Class Numbers can be easily constructed. For the construction of more complicated subjects, the original books *Colon classification* ed 6 and *Decimal classification* ed 16 are to be consulted. The schedule of main classes given in same chapter should be remembered.

CC	*Subject*	DC
	Library Science	
2	**Library science**	**02**
2:1	Book selection	025.21
2:2	Organisation	023
2:51	Classification	025.4
2:55	Cataloguing	025.3
2:6	Circulation work	025.6
2:7	Reference service	025.52
2:8	Administration	025
2:97	Documentation	
213	National central library	027.5
215	State central library	

22	Public library	027.4
221	Rural library	027.4223
222	City library	027.4222
23	Academic library	
232	Secondary school library	027.8223
233	College library	027.7
234	University library	027.7
261	Children's library	027.625

Mathematics

B	**Mathematics**	**51**
B0*b*	from special points of view	
B0*b*D	for Engineers	
B0*b*MY3	for Recreation	
B0*b*X	for Economists	
BO*b*X8	for Actuaries	
B11	Elementary arithmetic	511
B21	Elementary algebra	512
B23	Theory of equation	512.2
B28	**Statistics**	
B280b	from special points of view	
B280bJ	for Agriculturists	
B280bS	for Psychologists	
B280bT	for Educationists	
B280bX	for Economists	
B280bX8	for Actuaries	
B3	**Analysis**	
B32	Calculus	517
B321	Differential	517.2
B325	Integral	517.3
B5	Trigonometry	514
B52	Plane	514.5
B6	Geometry	

B6:5	Descriptive	515
B6:2	Plane	513.1
B622	Conies	516
B622:2	Analytical conies	513.22
B622:6	Geometrical conies	516
B63	Solid geometry	513.3
B7	**Mechanics**	**531**
B71	Solid	531
B71:1	Dynamics	531.3
B71:3	Statics	531.2
B75	Liquid	532
B75:2	Hydrodynamics	532.5
B75:3	Hydrostatics	532.2
B78:2	Aerodynamics	533.6
B9	**Astronomy**	**52**
B9.1	Chronology	529
B9:17	Calendar	529.3
B9:13	Era	529.2
B9:6	Astrophysics	532
B9:8	Cosmogony	523.1
B9:94	Nautical	527
B91	Earth	525
B92	Moon	523.3
B93	Sun	523.7
B94	Planet	523.4
B951	Meteor	523.5
B952	Comet	523.6
B96	Star	523.8

74C Physics

C	**Physics**	**53**
C15:(B1)	Mensuration	511.8
C:*f*3	Practical physics	530.765

C2	**Properties of matter**	
C21	Solid	
C216	Crystal	
C25	Liquid	
C25,4	Surface tension	532.6
C28	Gas	533
C28.76	Vacuum	
C3	**Sound**	**534**
C3:7	Accoustics	534.84
C4	Heat	536
C4:7	Thermodynamics	536.7
C5	**Radiation**	**535**
C5:3	Spectroscopy	535.84
C51	Light	535
C51:3	Spectroscopy of light	535.84
C52	Ultra-violet	535.844
C53	X-ray	537.535
C56	Infra-red ray	535.842
C57	Hertzian wave	
C6	**Electricity**	**537.2**
C6:45	Photo-electricity	537.54
C62	Current electricity	537.5
C7	**Magnetism**	**538**
C9B3	Nuclear physics	539.7
CM	Kinetic theory	530.13
CN	Relativity	530.11
CN1	Quantum theory	530.12
CN2	Wave Mechanics	530.12

74D Engineering

D	**Engineering**	**62**
Dl	Civil	

D2	Irrigation	
D3	Building	
D4	Transport (Track)	627.2
D411	High-way	
D514	Rail-road	
D416	Bridge	
D42:8	Harbour	627.2
D43:8	Aerodrome	
D5	**Transport (Vehicle)**	
D521	Cart	
D5125	Cycle	529.2272
D513	Motor	629.2
D515	Railway carriage	625.2
D525	Ship	625.824
D525	Sub-marine	623.825
D535	Aeroplane	629.1334
D58	Space vehicle	
D6	**Mechanical Engineering**	
D6:6	Machinery	
D6:7	General machinery	
D6:8	Machine tool	621.9
D6:9(D2:1)	Excavating machinery	624.156
D6:9(D85)	Pumping "	621.64
D6:9(M14)	Printing "	681.62
D6:9(M7)	Textile	677.0285
D6:9(MC421)	Refrigerating "	621.56
D6:9(MJ38)	Flouring "	521.92
D6:9(MJ381)	Rice husking "	
D62	**Principles of Mechanism**	**621.8**
D635	Hydraulic Engineering	621.2
D6351	Waterwheel	621.21
D6355	Water turbine	621.24

D638	Pneumatic Engineering	621.5
D6381	Wind mill	621.45
D6385	Turbine	
D6387	Compressed air	621.42
D64	**Heat Engine**	
D641	Steam engine	621.11
D645	Steam turbine	621.165
D646	Internal combustion engine	621.43
D6465	Oil engine	621.434
D6466	Diesel engine	621.436
D6467	Gas engine	621.434
D6468	Hot air engine	624,41
D65	**Electronics**	**621.381**
D65:4	Wireless	621.384
D65:43	Broadcasting	
D65:45	Television	621.338
D65:47	Telegraphy	621.3842
D65:48	Telephony	621.3845
D65:78	Servomechanism	
D66	**Electrical Engineering**	**621.3**
D664	Alternating current	621.3133
D665	Weak current	631.33
D665:45	Telegraphy	621.382
D665:48	Telephone	621.385
D7	**Nuclear Engineering**	**621.48**
D8	Sanitary Engineering	628
D85	Water supply	628.1
D855	Purification	628.16
D856	Distribution	628.14
D86	Sewage	628.3
D88	Municipal refuse	628.3

74E Chemistry

E	**Chemistry**	**54**
E:l	General	54
E:2	Physical	541
E :22	Solution	541.34
E :235	Colloid	541.345
E:24	Thermo-chemistry	541.36
E:25	Photo-chemistry	541.35
E:26	Electro-chemistry	541.37
E:28	Steoro-chemistry	541.6
E:3	**Analytical chemistry**	**543**
E:4	Synthesis	546.45
E:5	Extraction	547.2
E :8	Manipulation	
El	**Inorganic**	**546**
E2	Basic oxide	546.4
E3	Acid	546.24
E4	Salt	546.34
E5	**Organic**	**547**
E68	Carbohydrate	547.78
E6892	Starch	547.782
E6894	Cellulose	547.782
E7	Aromatic compound	547.6
E9	Biosubstance	547
E92	Alkaloid	547.72
E927	Protein	547.75
E94	Fat	547.438
E95	Pigmant	547.2
E97	Vitamin	547.74
E982	Enzyme	547.758
E986	Hormone	547.194
E9G	Biochemistry	547.192

	74F Technology	
F182	Iron	659.1
F191	**Metallurgy**	**669**
F4416	Enamel	666.2
F527	Celluloid	668.44
F53	Food	664
F54	Alcohol	663.1
F547	Wine	663.2
F548	Beer	664.4
F55	**Fuel**	**662.6**
F551	Coal	662.62
F555	Petroleum	665.5
F5552	Petrol	665.5
F5591	Matches	662.5
F5594	Explosive	662
F56	Drug	615.1
F573	Artificial silk	
F58	Dye	667.2
F5895	Paint	667.6
F594	Poison	
F9491	Candle	665.1
F9496	Soap	668.12
	74G Biology	
G	**Biology**	**57**
G:19	Microscopy	578
G:2	Morphology	574.4
G:3	Physiology	574.1
G :33	Metabolism	574.13
G:346	Fasting	613.24
G:394	Fatigue	612.816
G:5	Ecology	575.5
G:563	Parasitism	574.23

G :58	Migration	
G:6	**Genetics**	**575.1**
G :61	Heredity	575.11
G:64	Hybridisation	575.1
G:66	Evolution	575
G:67	Reproduction	574.16
G:7	Ontogeny (Growth)	575.6
Gl	Life	577.2
G11	Cell (Cytology)	574.87
G116	Gene	576.3
G12	Tissue (Histology)	574.82
	74 H Geology	
H	**Geology**	**55**
H:(C)	Geophysics	
H1	Mineralogy	549
H1:8	Crystallography	548
H19	Precious stone	553.8
H2	Petrology	552
H3	Structural geology	551.8
H36	Mountain formation	551.43
H4	**Physiography**	**551.4**
H411	Volcano	551.21
H4132	Earthquake	551.22
H6	Paleontology	56
H7	Economic geology	553
H7:15	Prospecting	622.1
H7:155	Occurrence	553
H7:16	Genesis	353
	741 Botany	
I	**Botany**	**58**
I:12	Flora	581.9

1:12.2	Indian flora	581.954
I:13	Popular description	
I:I3.2	Indian plants	
I:18	List	
I22	Algae	589.3
I23	Fungi	589.23
I2375	Mushroom	635.8
I32	Moss	588.2
I5	Flowering plants	583,584

Note: Each of the classes 122 to 15 may be divided as G:2 to G:7 and 1:12 to 1:18. For example,

123:3	Physiology of fungi	
	74J Agriculture	
J	**Agriculture**	**J**
J:l	Soil	631.4
J:2	Manure	641.86,
J:2:25	Compositing	631.875
J:24	Chemical manure (Fertilizer)	631.82
J:241	Potassic	631.83
J:245	Nitrogenous	631.84
J :246	Phosphatic	631.85
J:3	Propagation method	631.53
J:4	Disease	632
J:5	Crop development	631.54
J :7	Harvesting	631.55
J:97	Utilisation	
J1	Horticulture	635
J16	Floriculture	63
J2	Feed crop	635
J3	**Food crop**	**633**
J311	Sugarcane	
J321	Onion	635.25
J341	Potato	633.491

J3513	Cabbage	635.34
J37	**Fruit Culture**	**634**
J371	Apple	634.11
J372	Orange	634.31
J3731	Plantain	634.773
J374	Grape	634.8
J3751	Mango	634.441
J3752	Pine apple	
J38	**Cereal**	**633.1**
J381	Rice	633.18
J382	Wheat	633.11
J385	Corn	
J397	Millet	633.17
J388	Pulse	
J389	Nut	
J451	Tea	633.72
J456	Tobacco	633.71
J481	Coffee	633.71
J581	Groundnut	
J582	Coconut	
J641	Cinchona	
J671	Black pepper	633.841
J674	Chillies	
J711	Rubber	634.9865
J741	Jute	633.34
J742	Flax	633.52
J743	Hemp	632.53
J781	Cotton	633.51
J9D	Dry farming	631.586
J9S	Soilless farming	
JB	Forestry	634.9

Note: Each of the classes from Jl to JB may be further subdivided on the analogy of the subdivision of bare J. For example,

J381:7	Harvesting of rice	
J451:4	Disease of tea-plant	
JB:97	Forest utilisation	634.92727
	74K Zoology	
K	**Zoology**	**59**
K:12	Fauna	591
K:12.2	Indian fauna	591.954
K:13	Description	
K.13.2	India	
K:2	Morphology	591.4
K:3	Physiology	591.1
K:5	Ecology	591.5
K:58	Migration	591.52
K:73	Embryology	593
K1	Invertebrate	592
K6	Worm	595.1
K7	Mollusc	594
K86	Insect	595.7
K9	Vertebrate	596
K92	Fish	597
K93	Amphibian	597.6
K94	Reptile	598
K96	Bird	598.2
K97	Mammal	599

Note: Each of the classes K1 to K97 may be divided as bare K, for example, (K96:58 Bird migration)

	74KB Animal Husbandry	
KZ	**Animal Husbandry**	**636**
KZ:4	Veterinary science	636
KZ31	Dairy	637
KZ31:71	Milk	637.1

KZ31:73	Butter	637.2
KZ332	Fishery	639.3
KZ35	Poultry	636.5
KZ442	Horse	636.1
KZ54	**Pet Animal**	**636**
KZ54I	Dog	636.7
KZ542	Cat	636.8
KZ611	Bee	638.1
KZ771	Silkworm	638.2
	74 L Medicine	
L	**Medicine**	**61**
LZ	Pharmocognacy	
L:13	Nursing Home	321.16
L:14	Hospital	36l.ll
L:15	Sanatorium	362.13
L:2	Morphology	611
L:3	Physiology	612
L:4	**Disease**	**616**
L:4:l	Nursing	610.72
L:4:2	Etiology	616
L:4:3	Diagnosis	616.075
L:4:4	Pathology	616.07
L:4:5	Prevention	614.44
L:4:6	**Treatment**	**615**
L:4:6253	Treatment by X-Ray	616.8422
L:4:63	Treatment by drug	615.7
L:4:6426	Fast cure	615.85
L:4:65	Hydro-therapy	615.853
L:4:66	Antibody and serum therapy	615.37
L:5:68	Aero·therapy	615.836
L:4:7	**Surgery**	**617**
L:4:8	Diet regulation	615.854
L:4:9I	After care	

L:4:97	First aid	614.88
L:42	**Infectious disease**	**616.9**
L:421	Tuberculosis	616.995
L:423	Virus disease	616.92
		616.91
L:4537	Allergy	615.97
L:4725	Cancer	616.994
L:473	Hernia	617.559
L:473:7	Operation for hernia	617,559
L:475	Abcess	617.2
L:49	Burns	617.11
L:491:97	First aid for burns	617.11

Note: Each specific disease may be further divided as "General disease L:4", as illustrated under Hernia and Burns.

L:5	**Public health**	**614**
L:51	Vital statistics	312
L:521	Habitation	613.5
L:522	Animal	636.0894
L:523	Food	614.31
L:54	Preventive measure	614.44
L:55	Public hygiene	614.7
L:57	**Personal hygiene**	**613**
L:571	Residence	613.5
L:572	Recreation	613.7
L:573	Food	613.2
L:573	Stimulant	613.8
L:575	Toilet	646.7
L:577	Clothing	
L:578	Sleep	613.79
L:8	Physical fitness	
LI	Regional organs	

L12:46	Obesity	616.398
L177	Throat	
L183	**Ear**	
L183:4	Disease of the ear	617.3
L813:4:7	Surgery of the ear	617.8
L185	**Eye**	
L185:4	Disease of the eye	617.7
L192	Joints	
L192:415	Rheumatism	616.991
L2	Digestive system	
L214	Teeth	
L25	**Intestines**	
L25:4241	Typhoid	616.9272
L25:4251	Cholera	616.932
L25:4372	Hookworm disease	616.9654
L25:451	Constipation	616.34
L25:452	Diarrhoea	616.34
L29 1:453	Jaundice	616.365
L293:62	Diabetes	616.46
L3	**Circulatory system**	
L32	Heart	
L32:4	Disease of heart	616.12
L35:4I1	Anaemia	616.936
L35:4261	Malaria	616.9362
L39:481	Elephantiasis	616.9652
L396:4241	Plague	616.9232
L4	**Respiratory system**	
L4:4241	Influenza	616.203
L4:4242	Whooping cough	616.204
L41	Nose	
L41 :4241	Diphtheria	616.9313
L44:415	Bronchitis	616.23
L44:453	Asthma	616.23

L45:421	Pulmonary tuberculosis	616.246
L45:424	Pneumonia	616.241
L62:4261	Kala-azar	
L6	**Ductless glands**	
L.62:5261	Kala-azar	
L7	**Nervous system**	
L7:51	Neurasthenia	616.343
L7:52	Insomnia	616.849
L72	Brain	
L72:453	Epilepsy	616.353
L73	Spinal cord	
L73:4241	Titanus	616.9318
L77:411	Paralysis	616.842
L82	Bone	
L82:463	Ricket	616.95
L87	Skin	
L87:4	Skin disease	616.5
L9A	**Specials**	
L9B	Embryology	
L9C	Child medicine	618.92
L9F	Female medicine	618
L95:3	Obstetrics	618.2
L95:4	Gynaecology	618.1
L9H	Tropical medicine	
L9X	Industrial medicine	
LA	**Systems**	
LB	Ayurveda medicine	615.89
LB.xl,l	Charaka Samhita	
L B:4:7.x2,l	Susruta Samhita	
LB:68;x 1,1	Vagbhata Raseratna samuccya	
LC	Sidda medicine	615.89
LD	Unani medicine	615.89
LL	Homoeopathy	615.532

LM	Naturopathy	615,535
L:Z	**Pharmocognacy**	**615**
L:Z3	Pharmocology	615.1
L:Z5	Materia medica	615.1
L:Z8	Pharmacy	615.4

*Note;*1. Any class from L1 to L87 can be divided as bare L is divided from L: 11 to L:491.

Examples

L44:415:3	Diagnosis of bronchitis	616.23075

2. Any of the systems LB to LM may be divided as L:l to L9H. The one extra prescription is this. If any of the organ divisions from "1 Regional organ" to "87 Skin" is to be added, the organ numbers 1to 87, whichever it be, is to be preceded by a comma. Similarly, if any of the divisions "9B Embryology" to "9X Industrial medicine" is to be added, this number whichever it be, is to be preceded by a comma.

Examples

LB,185:4:6	Ayurvedic treatment for eye disease	615.89
LB,9F:4	Ayurvedic gynaecology	615.89
LL,9C,44:453:63	Homeopathic drug remedy for asthma in child	615.532

3. See colon classification Part 3 Chapter L for Indian classics in Medicine.

Useful Arts

CC	*Subject*	*DC*
M	Useful Arts	6
Ml	**Book production**	**655**
M13	Paper making	676
M14	Printing	655

M144	Book illustration	
M15	Binding	615.7
M3	Home science	64
M3:3	Cooking	641.5
M4	Smithy	682
M5	Carpentry	694
M6	Glass industry	666.1
M7	**Textiles**	**677**
M7:l	Spinnin	677.02822
M7:2	Weaving	677.02824
M71	Cotton	677.21
M72	Wool	677. 31
M73	Silk	677.4
M8	Tailoring	687.1
M92	Masonry	693
M95	Photography	77
M98	Packaging	658.7884
MJ7	Ropemaking	677.71
MY1	**Physical training**	**796**
MY11	Callisthenics	796.41
MY12	Heavy exercise	796.43
MY13	Gymnastics	796.4
MY2	Athletics	796
MY2121	Football	796.33
MY2131	Tennis	796.34
MY2132	Badminton	796.34
MY2141	Cricket	796.358
MY22	Competitive sport	796.07
MY25	Aquatic sport	797
MY251	Swimming	797.2
MY3	Indoor game	793
MY3I	Card play	795.4
MY4	Jugglery	793.5

MY5	Animal racing	798.8
MY6	Hunting	799.2
MY7	Scouting	360.43
MY974	Stamp collection	383.22

D 74 Spiritual experience and mysticism

Δ	Spiritual experience and mysticism	189.5
Δ :34	Breath control	
Δ :8	Occultism	133
Δ ,16:8	Spiritualism	133.9
Δ :86	Prophecy	133.3
Δ :862	Physiognomy	138
Δ :8627	Palmistry	133.6
Δ :8628	Phrenology	139
Δ :864	Astrology	133.5
Δ :8692	Omen	133.3
Δ :87	Magic and witchcraft	133.4
Δ 2	**Hindu yoga**	
2x4	Yoga Upanishads	
Δ 22	Hatha	
Δ 23	Jnana	
Δ 24	Karma	
Δ 25	Bhakti	
Δ 26	Raja	
Δ 28	Siddha	

74N Fine Arts

N	Fine Arts	7
NA	Architecture	72
NB	Town planning	711.4
NC	Plastic art	
ND	Sculpture	73
ND,9(Q)	Iconography	73
NJ	Inlay art	745.51

NL	Embroidery	746
NM	Graphic art	76
NN	Engraving	
NP	Drawing	74
NQ	Painting	75
NR	Music	78
NR;2	**Wind instrument**	**786**
NR;21	Pipe	788.9
NR;22	Flute	788.5
NR;291	Harmonium	786.94
NR;3	**Stringed instrument**	
NR;31	Vina	787
NR;32	Violin	787.1
NR;34	Piano	786.2
NR;4	**Percussion instrument**	**789**
NR;41	Drum	789.1
NR;91	**Vocal music**	**784**
NR,92	Dramatic music	782
NR,93	Orchestral music	785.1
NR44	**Indian music**	
NR441	Carnatic music	781.7548
NR445	Hindustani music	781.7541
NR5	**European music**	
NS	**Dance**	**793.3**
NT	**Theatre**	**792**
NU	Puppet play	791.53
NV	Shadow play	791.5
NW	Cinema	791.43
NX	Talkie	791.43

Note: See Colon Classification Part 3 Chapter N for Indian classics in Music.

Literature

Note: For definiteness, English is taken in the following schedule as the favoured language of the library.

O	English literature	82
O-,1	English poetry	821
O-,1K08	John Milton	821.47
O-,1K08,6	Paradise lost	821.47
O-,1L88	Alexander Pope	821.53
O-,1M09	Alfred Tennyson	821.81
O-,IL08	Elizabeth Barret Browning	821.82
O-,IM12	Robert Browning	821.83
O-,1M61	Rabindranath Tagore	821.91
O-,1M841	John Drinkwater	821.91
O-,1M851	Ezra Pound	82.91
O-,2	English Drama	822
O-,2J64	William Shakespeare	822.33
O-,2J64.5	Tragedies of Shakespeare	822.33
O-2J64.51	Hamlet	822.33
O-,2J64,5l:g	Criticism of Hamlet	822.33
O-,2L51	Sheroidian	822.65
O-,2M57	Bernard Shaw	822.91
O-2M60	James Barrie	821.91
O-2N09	Stephen Spender	821.91
0-,3	English fiction	823
O-,3L7I	Walter Scott	823.73
O-,3M11	William Makepeace Thackeray	824.82
O-,3M12	Charles Dickens	823.3
0-,3M20	George Elliot	823.89
O-,3M40	Thomas Hardy	823.89
O-,3M64	Rudyard Kipling	823.91
O-,3N09	Stephen Spender	823.91
0-,4	English essays	824

O15	Sanskrit literature	891.2
O15,1	Sanskrit poetry	891.21
O15,1D60	Kalidasa	891.21
O15,1F60	Jayadeva	891.21
O15,2	Sanskrit drama	891.22
O15,2D35	Bhasa	891.22
O15,2D40	Kalidasa	891.22
O15,2D42	Dinnaga	891.22
O15,2D60	Harsha	891.22
O15,2D70	Bhavabhuti	891.22
O15,2D63	Murari	891.22
O15,2M97	Mahalingasastri	891.22
O152	Hindi literature	891.43
O152,1	Hindi poetry	891.43
O152,1J32	Tulsi Das	891.43

*Note:*1. The above are only illustrations of class numbers in the main class "O Literature".

2. The Colon Number for any work in literature can be got by the facet formula:

   O [Language], [Form] [Author], [Work]

3. The language for the language facet is the language in which, the author – poet, dramatist etc. – wrote his work. The isolate number in the language facet is to be got from the schedule of language isolates in section "Language Isolates".

4. The form number is to be got from the following schedule:

1.	Poetry	4 Literature in the form of letters
2.	Drama	5 Prose
3.	Fiction	6 Campu

5. The author number — that is, the isolate number in the author facet — that is, the number to denote the author of the poem, drama, fiction etc. as the case may be—is to be got by the Chronological Device. In other words, the name of the author is normally represented by the year of his birth, translated into isolate number in accordance with the schedule of time isolates. The year of birth is easily got from books in the history of literature concerned or from *Who's Who*.

However, we do not have sufficient help to find the year of birth of the authors in Indian literature. It is particularly so with modern authors. This is due to the absence of a good *Who's Who* for living Indian authors. But in all cases, at least the century of birth of the author may be guessed. Then, the author number, in such cases, may be made of the century digit followed by the first letter of the name of the author. If the names of several authors of the same century in the same form of literature in the same language, begin with the same letter, in the case of the second of them the second letter in the name may also be added in capital. And so on. For example,

Example

CC	*Subject*	*DC*
O31,3NS	Seetharaman, Tamil novelist born in the twentieth century	
O31,3NSU	Subramanian, another Tamil novelist born in the twentieth century	
O31,3NSUN	Sundaram, a third Tamil novelist born in the twentieth century	
O31,3NV	Vaidyanathan, Tamil novelist born in the twentieth century	

O31,3NVE	Venkatachalam, another Tamil novelist born in the twentieth century

6. The work number — that is, the isolate number in the work facet of a particular author — may be fixed serially as 1, 2, 3, ... 10, 11, 12, etc.
7. The class numbers for ancient Tamil works are given in Chapter O of Part 3 of Colon Classification.

The class numbers for some Marathi authors are given in the *Dvibhindu-vargikarena* by R S Parkhi.

The class numbers for some Hindi authors are given in the *Granthalaya Prakriya* by Ranganathan and Nagar.

CC	*Subject*	*DC*
	74P Linguistics	
Note: In what follows, English is taken as the favoured language.		
P	Linguistics	4
P-	English linguistics	42
P-,D	Old English	429
P-,E	Middle English	42
P-,J	Modern English	42
P-,J:1	Phonetics of modern English	421
P-,J:2	Morphology "	425.1
P-,J:3	Syntax "	425.2
P-,J:4/k	Dictionary "	423
P-,J:7	Composition in "	808
P15	Sanskrit linguistics	491.2
P15,A	Vedic grammar	491.2
P15,C	Classical Sanskrit	491.2
P15.Cxl,l	Panini	491.2
P15,Cx1,1,2	Pantanjali	491.2

*Note:*1. The class numbers for the linguistics of the other languages are to be constructed on the above model, inserting after P the number of the language concerned, as found in the Language Isolate Schedule given in section "Language Isolates".

2. Class numbers for the classics in Indian linguistics is given in Chapter P of Part 3 of Colon Classification.

CC	*Subject*	*DC*
	74Q Religion	
Q	Religion	2
Q:1	Mythology	291.13
Q:2	Scripture	291.82
Q:25	Sayings	
Q:26	Traditions	291.83
Q:3	**Theology**	**2**
Q:31	God	211
Q:311	Avatara	
Q:315	Avasara	
Q:321	Angel	291.215
Q:324	Devil	291.216
Q:33	Founder of religion	
Q:4	**Religious practices**	**217**
Q:41	Personal	
Q:417	Namavali	
Q:418	Sacred formula	
Q:4192	Ritual	291.38
Q:4198	Pilgrimage	291.38
Q:42	Sacrament	
Q:43	Holi day	291.36
Q:45	**Public worship**	**291.3**
Q:494	Sacrifice	291.34
Q:495	Holy water	

Q:6	Religious institution	291.65
Q:7	Religious sect formation	
Q1	**Hinduism (Vedic)**	**294.1**
Q1:21	Samhita	
Q1:22	Brahmana	
Q1:23	Aranyaka	
Q1:24	Upanishad	
Q1:4	Kalpa sutra	
Q11	**Rig Vedic religion**	
Q111	Aitreyin	
Q112	Kausatakin	
Q112:22	Sankhayana Brahmana	
Q12	**Yajur Vedic religion**	
Q121	Black	
Q125	Taittiriya	
Q 125:24	Ekagni-kanda (Mantra-prasna) (Mantra-pata)	
Q125:25	Narayana Upanishad	
Q125:26	Swetaswatara Upanishad	
Q127	Madnyandina	
Q127:22	Satapata Brahmana	
Q127:24	Brahad-aranyaka Upanishad	
Q127:25	Isavasya Upanishad	
Q13	Sama Vedic religion	
Q131	Tandin	
Q131:22	Chandogya Brahmana	
Q131:24	Chandogya Upanishad	
Q132	Talavakara	
Q 132:24	Kena Upanishad	
Q14	Atharva Vedic religion	
Q14:22	Gopaa Brahmana	
Q 141	Saunakiya	
Q141:24	Prasna Upanishad	

Q141:25	Manduka Upanishad	
Q141.26	Mandukya Upanishad	
Q2	**Hinduism (post-Vedic)**	**294.5**
Q21	**Smartaism**	
Q21:21.x1	Purusha-suktam	
Q21:22	Smarta Puranas	
Q21:221	Brahma Purana	
Q21:222	Markandeya Purana	
Q21:223	Bhavishya Purana	
Q21:2231	Bhavishyottara Purana	
Q21:224	Vamana Purana	
Q21:225	Brahmanda Purana	
Q2I:2251	Adhyatma Ramayana	
Q21:2252	Rama Gita	
Q21:226	Yogavasishta Ramayana (Jnana Vasishta)	
Q21:227	Ananda Ramayana	
Q21:228	Adbhuta Ramayana	
Q22	**Vaishnavism**	
Q22 *wx* 1,1	Mahipati: Bhakta-vijayam	
Q22 *wx* 1,2	Mahipati: Bhakta-lilamrita	
Q22 wx 2	Chandradatta: Bhakta-mala	
Q22:22	Vaishnara Puranas	
Q22.-22	Padma Purana	
Q22:2211	Siva Gita	
Q22:222	Vishnu Purana	
Q22:223	Bhagavata Purana	
Q22:224	Narada Purana	
Q22:2241	Narada Upa-Purana	
Q22:225	Brahma Vaivarta Purana	
Q22:226	Varaha Purana	
Q22:227	Garuda Purana	
Q22:2271	Vishnu-dharmottara	
Q22:228	Hari-vamsa Purana	

Q22:2291	Kalki Purana
Q22:2292	Narasimha Purana
Q22:2293	Bhargava Purana
Q22:417.xl	Nalayira Prabanda
Q22:4173xl	Vishnu-shasranama
Q23	**Saivism**
Q23wxl	Sekkizhar: Periya-puranam
Q23:21x1	Rudra
Q23:21x2	Camaka
Q23:22	**Saiva Puranas**
Q23:221	Vayu Purana
Q23:222	Agni Purana
Q23:223	Linga Purana
Q23:224	Ganesa Purana
Q23:2244	Ganesa Gita
Q23:225	Matsya Purana
Q23:226	Skandapurana
Q23:226	Suta Samhita
Q23:227	Kurma Purana
Q23:2271	Iswara Gita
Q23:228	Saura Purana
Q23:2291	Siva Purana
Q23:417xl	Tevaram
Q232	Agamic Saivaism
Q233	Kashmir Saivaism
Q234	Vira Saivaism
Q24	**Ganapatyism**
Q25	**Saktaism**
Q25x 1,1	Sankara : Saundarya-laheri
Q25:21x5	Srisuktam
Q25:21 *x6*	Durga-suktam
Q25:22	**Sakta Puranas**

Q25:221	Devi Bhagavata	
Q25:222	Brihad-dharma Purana	
Q25:223	Kalika Purana	
Q25:225	Lalitopakhyana	
Q25:2291	Devi-mahatmya	
Q25:4173xl	Lalita-sahasra-nama	
Q26	Shanmukaism	
Q28	Sauraism	
Q28:22	**Saura Puranas**	
Q28:221	Aditya Purana	
Q28:222	Samba Purana	
Q3	Jainism	294 .4
Q31	Swetambara	
Q31:211	Anga	
Q31:212	Upanga	
Q31:213	Prakirna	
Q31:2I6	Mula-sutra	
Q32	Digambara	
Q4	Buddhism	294.3
Q41	Hinayana	294.31
Q41:2	Tripitaka	294.30032
Q42	Mahayana	294.32
Q5	**Judaism**	**296**
Q6	**Christianity**	**2**
Q6:21	Bible	22
Q6:22	Old Testament	221
Q6.23	New Testament	225
Q7	**Mohammadanism**	**297**
Q7:21	Quran	297.12

Note: More detailed divisions of the different religions will be found in the original Colon Classification.

CC	*Subject*	*DC*
	74R Philosophy	
R	Philosophy	1
R1	Logic	16
R11	Inductive Logic	161
R12	Deductive Logic	162
R2	Epistemology	121
R3	**Metaphysics**	**11**
R4	**Ethics**	**17**
R4,(Q2)	Hindu ethics	
R5	Esthetics	111.85
R6	**Indian philosophy**	**181 .4**
R61	Hindu philosophy	
R621	Vaisashika	181.44
R625	Nyaya	181.43
R631	Sankhya	181.41
R635	Yoga	181.45
R64	Purva mimamsa	181.42
R641	Bhatta mimamsa	
R645	Prabhakara mimamsa	
R65	**Vedanta**	**181.48**
R65.0	Upanishads	
R65,271	Brahadaranyaka	
R65,31	Chandogya	
R65,5	Brahma-sutra	
R65,6	Bhagavad Gita	
R66	**Advaita**	
R663	Pratyabigna	
R67	Visishta-advaita	
R672	Vaishnava	
R673	Saiva-siddhanta	
R68	**Dvaita**	

Note: R66 to R68 may be divided on the analogy of R65.

R69	Other Indian systems
R 691	Charvaka philosophy
R693	Jaina philosophy
R694	Buddhistic philosophy

Note: A full list of the Indian systems of philosophy and of the classics in them is given in Chapter R of Part 3 of Colon Classification.

74S Psychology

S	Psychology	15
O bT	For teachers	
S:2	Sensation	152
S:31	Attention	152.723
S:34	Work	158.7
S:344	Fatigue	158.7
S:4	Cognition	153
S:43	Memory	154
S:44	Reasoning	153.6
S:47	Opinion	301.154
S:5	Emotion	157
S:6	Conation	158
S:7	Personality	137
S:72	Intelligence	151
S:73	Ability	137.38
S:74	Character	137
S:75	Temperament	137.42
S:76	Intuition	156
S:78	Psychic powers	
S:791	Longevity	
S:793	Endurance	
S:794	Immunity	
S:796	Drug habit	132.73
S:8	Meta-psychology	13
S:81	Sleep	135.2

S:811	Dream	135.3
3:813	Hallucination	134.52
S:815	Subconscious	153.8
S:851	Hypnotism	134
S:852	Suggestion	
S:8521	Auto-suggestion	134.6
S1	Child	136.7
52	Adolescent	136.7354
S35	Middle age	136.52
S3S	Old age	136.53
S4	Vocational (to be divided by subject device)	

Examples

S4(NR)	Psychology of musicians	
S4(0,l)	Psychology of poets	
S4(Z)	Psychology of lawyers	
S51	Male	136.16
S55	Female	136.15
S6	Abnormal	
S7	Race	36.4
S8	Social	301.15
S91	Animal	151.3

5

Cataloguing in Practice

"As tools become rusty, so does the mind; a garden uncared for soon becomes smothered in weeds; a talent neglected withers and dies."

—**Miguel de Cervantes**

Before proceeding to practical cataloguing we will reproduce the Five Laws of Library Science propounded by S.R. Ranganathan.

Five Laws of Library Science

Noted scholar, Dr. Shiyali Ramamrita Ranganathan is known as the "the father of library science in India," and respected by librarians all over the world. He proposed five laws of library science. Many librarians worldwide accept them as the foundations of their philosophy (e.g. Koehler et al., 2000)

These laws are:

1. Books are for use.
2. Every reader his [or her] book.
3. Every book its reader.
4. Save the time of the User.
5. The library is a growing organism.

Basically, the Five Laws of Library Science are some of the most influential concepts in that field. Since they were published in 1931, these five laws "have remained a centerpiece of professional values..." These basic theories of Library Science continue to directly affect the development of this discipline and the service of all libraries.

S.R. Ranganathan's early education was of a mathematics background. This systematic way of thinking, he later applied to his work in library science, most notably his work on library classification and administration. (Indian Statistical Institute Library, et al. 2007) He went abroad to study librarianship at the University College of London, working under the renowned W.C. Berwick Sayers, and returned to India as a man possessed. He lived and breathed librarianship for the rest of his long and remarkable career. "From the middle of the nineteenth century, librarians in the west felt the need and started emphasizing the importance of enhanced services to library patrons. Formulation of the Five Laws of Library Science at long last, provided a solid and lasting foundation in this direction." (Kabir 2003)

First Law: *Books are for Use:* The 1st law of library science is "Books are for use' Which implies that a book should be durable & the material of which it is made should have longevity. The 1st law insists upon intensifying the use of books by every possible method and it urges the library profession to select such edition of the book which is readable & pleasing to the eye. A book is to select for easy understanding by the majority of the user of the library.A book that is written with flair for simple style, language & clarity of expression should be purchased...

The 1st law of library science is "Books are for use', which implies that the main task of a library is to circulate books to its users (rather than to protect and conserve books). Towards this end any obstacle should be removed as far as it is possible, making it as easy for a user to obtain a book, as it can be achieved. Obviously, losing a book for whatever reason makes it impossible for readers to use it, thus making the protection and preservation of book a means of fulfilling this law. Nevertheless, making a book accessible to readers is the primary goal. This law may be seen as the main (perhaps the only) law, for which the next laws are merely commentaries.

Second Law: ***Books are for All***—Any patron from the library community should have access to the books in the library. Any person has a right to use the collections housed in the library. There are not certain books or collections that some audiences within the population can not access. Collections should be developed that every part of the population will be interested in.

Third Law: ***Every Book Its Reader***—This law is about items in the library's collection, and who uses them. Each book in the library has a member of the community that will find the book useful or interesting. One of the major developments that Ranganathan contributed through this law is the idea that if a book is not being used often it needs exposure to groups of readers who will find it useful. On the other side it says it the responsibility of the librarian to make the book reachable to the users. This task includes several techniques like appropriate classification and cataloguing that help in identifying the needed book in the quick and efficient manner.In general it is all about the need of keeping the library in a well organised status.

Fourth Law: ***Save the Time of the Reader***—This law makes it clear that if readers find what they are looking for in a timely manner they will be more satisfied, and more likely to feel like their needs have been met. This not only makes library service more efficient, but also makes the reader feel like their search has been an effective one. The same time it is also concerned with the time that the library professional spends to serve the user. The is a stress on saving the library staff also.

Fifth Law: ***The Library is a Growing Organism***—This law says that the library is dependent on life and change. Without the human and organizational changes that occur, the library would neither function properly nor meet its purpose. Going further, it says that the library is something that grows for ever in accordance with contemporary technologies. In general it is like a growing kid.

Variants

In 1998, librarian Michael Gorman (past president of the American Library Association, 2005-2006), recommended the following laws in addition to Ranganathan's five in his small book, "Our Singular Strengths":

1. Libraries serve humanity.
2. Respect all forms by which knowledge is communicated.
3. Use technology intelligently to enhance service.
4. Protect free access to knowledge.
5. Honor the past and create the future.

In 2004, librarian Alireza Noruzi recommended applying Ranganathan's laws to the web in his paper, "Application of Ranganathan's Laws to the Web":

1. Web resources are for use.
2. Every user has his or her web resource.

3. Every web resource its user.
4. Save the time of the user.
5. The Web is a growing organism.

AACR2

AACR2 stands for the Anglo-American Cataloguing Rules, Second Edition. It is published jointly by the American Library Association, the Canadian Library Association, and the Chartered Institute of Library and Information Professionals (in the UK). AACR2 is designed for use in the construction of catalogues and other lists in general libraries of all sizes. The rules cover the description of, and the provision of access points for, all library materials commonly collected at the present time.

Despite the claim to be 'Anglo-American', the first edition of AACR was published in 1967 in somewhat distinct North American and British texts. The second edition of 1978 unified the two sets of rules (adopting the British spelling 'cataloguing') and brought them in line with the International Standard Bibliographic Description. Libraries wishing to migrate from the previous North American text were obliged to implement 'desuperimposition', a substantial change in the form of headings for corporate bodies.

AACR2 exists in several print versions, as well as an online version. Print versions are available from the publishers. The online version is available only via Cataloger's Desktop from the Library of Congress. Various translations are also available from other sources.

Principles of AACR include cataloguing from the item 'in hand' rather than inferring information from external sources and the concept of the 'chief source of information' which is preferred where conflicts exist.

As well as occasional minor amendments, a broader revision is under way with a view to a new edition in which the rules are more consistent and coherent, informed by the Functional Requirements for Bibliographic Records. This 'AACR3' has the working title 'Resource Description and Access'.

Function of Catalogue

The function of a catalogue is to provide to readers answers to questions such as the following:

1. Is there a book in the library by such and such an author ?

11. What are all the books in the library by him ?

2. Is there a book in the library with such and such a title — that is, name ?

3. Is there a book in the library with such and such a collaborator— that is, editor,translator, reviser, compiler, commentator, etc ? 31 What are all the books in the library with him as collaborator?

4. Is there a book in the library in such and such a publisher's series ?

41. What are all the books in the library in that publisher's series ?

5. Is there a book in the library in such and such a subject ?

51. What are all the books in the library on that subject and on its subdivisions and on subjects of which it is a subdivision?

Note: The examples of entries in this part are numbered serially for convenience of reference.

Author Entry

A catalogue has author entries to answer question 1. An Author Entry has the name of the author at its very beginning:

Example

1. Ranganatha (Shiyali Ramamrita) (1892).
   Library manual. Ed 2. 22 N60

Consolidated Author Entry

A catalogue has consolidated author entries to answer question 11. A Consolidated Author Entry has the name of an author its beginning. It gives after it all the books of the author in the library.

Example

2. Ranganathan (Shiyali Ramamrita) (1892).

Classified catalogue code. Ed 4.	2:55N N58
Colon classification. Ed 6.	2:51N3N60
Five laws of library science. Ed 2.	2N57
Library manual. Ed 2.	22 N60
Reference service and bibliography.	2:7 N40

Title Entry

A catalogue has title entries to answer question 2. A Title Entry has the title of the book at its very beginning.

Example

3. Hermes.
   By Jones. Evl.N3 N28

Collaborator Entry

A catalogue has collaborator entries to answer question

3. A Collaborator Entry has the name of the collaborator at its very beginning.

Example

4. Crookes (William) (1832), *Tr* and *Ed*.
   Wagner: Chemical technology. F N04

Series Entry

A catalogue has series entries to answer question 4. A Series Entry has the name of the publisher's series at its very beginning.

Consolidated Series Entry

A catalogue has consolidated series entries to question 41. A Consolidated Series Entry is a series entry giving in a serial sequence all the books of the series available in the library.

Example

5. Ranganathas series in library science.
   1 Kaula, *Ed:* Library movement in India.
   2.2.N5 N58
   2 Ranganatha: Classified catalogue code. Ed 4.
   2:55N N58
   3 Ranganathas Library administration. Ed 2.
   2:3 N59

Subject Entry

A catalogue has subject entries to answer question 5. A Subject Entry has the name of a subject at its very beginning.

Consolidated Subject Entry

A catalogue has consolidated subject entries to answer

question 51. A Consolidated Subject Entry is a subject entry giving in rough alphabetical sequence all the books in the subject available in the library.

Example

6. Botany

Coulter: Text-book of botany. 2 V.	I N10.1-.2
Sabesan: Intermediate botany.	1 N37
Warburg: Planzenwelt. 3 B.	I 113N 13.1-3

Subject Analytical Entry

If a subject is treated only in a part of a book, it is brought to the notice of readers by a Subject Analytical Entry. It too answers question 5. It specifies the part, the chapter, the section, on the pages of the book, containing the subject.

Example

7. Reference Seslvice.

   Ranganathan: Library manual. Part 3. 22 N60

Call Number Entry

The very beginning of an entry in a catalogue may have the call number of a book instead of the name of its subject. It too answers question 5. It is called Call Number Entry. This is an alternative to subject entry.

Example

8. 22N60 Ranganathan (Shiyali Ramamrita) (1892).

   Library manual for Library Authorities, librarians, and honorary library workers. Ed 2.

   (Ranganathan series in library science, 6)

   (Madras Library Association, publication series, 25).

Cross Reference Entry

If a subject is treated only in a part of a book, it is brought to the notice of readers by a Cross Reference Entry. It too answers question 5. It specifies the part, the chapter, the section, or the pages of the book, containing the subject. The class number of the subject occurs at the very beginning of such an entry. This is an alternative to subject analytical entry.

There are two important types of catalogue. They are:

1. Classified catalogue; and
2. Dictionary catalogue.

Their essential difference is in respect of subject entries. In the classified catalogue, all the subject entries, including subject-analytical entries, are arranged together by their respective class numbers. This enables the classified catalogue to answer question 51 quite easily. In the dictionary catalogue, the subject entries, including subject-analytical entries, are scattered alphabetically by the names of the subjects. Another difference is main entry — that is, the entry giving the largest amount of information about the book and forming the chief source of all the other brief added entries. In the classified catalogue, the call number entry is made the main entry. In the dictionary catalogue, the author entry is made the main entry.

Example

1. The entry 8 in section 8153 is the main entry of this book; for classified catalogue.
2. The following is its main entry for dictionary catalogue.

10. Ranganathan (Shiyali Ramamrita) (1892).

Library manual for Library Authorities, librarians and honorary library workers. Ed 2.

(Ranganathan series in library science, 5).

(Madras Library Association, publication series, 25). 22 N59.

135,791.

See also Entries

A reader, looking for books on a particular subject, looks up the name of the subject entries. Usually, hardly any reader is able to name his precise subject. He generally mentions a subject of greater extension — that is, a broad subject having his precise subject as a subdivision. For example, suppose the precise subject sought by a reader is "Drinking vessel in use among gypsies". The reader may say, "I wish to have a book on 'Gypsies' ". He may even mention "Ethnology" or simply "Sociology". Some may perhaps be a little more precise and mention "Equipment of gypsies". To help readers in all such contingencies, the dictionary catalogue should give direction from each such broad subject to his precise subject. Such an entry is called a *See also* Entry.

Class Index Entry

In the case of the Classified Catalogue, the reader will not know the number either of his precise subject or of any of the six broader subjects mentioned in the entries of section 8161. He should therefore be helped by an entry to find the class number of each of the subjects mentioned by him. Such an entry is called a Class Index Entry. The following class index entries will therefore be necessary, in the case under consideration.

Example

Note: For brevity, *"see"* is used as the directing element.

> The full directing element prescribed is "For books in this class and its subclasses, see the Classified Part of the catalogue under the "Class Number".

Recommendation

The Classified Catalogue is recommended for adoption. Charles Ammi Cutter, the pioneer in catalogue, wrote, "It is true that by following up all the references of a dictionary catalogue under Theology, for example, a man may construct for himself a list of the theological literature in the library; but to do this requires time and mental effort, and it is characteristic of the desultory reader that he is averse to mental effort. What is wanted by him and by the busy man when now and then he has the same object, is to find the titles from which he could select brought together within the compass of a few pages". All this implies that Cutter preferred the classified catalogue, because it answers question 51 in a better way than the dictionary catalogue. But he could not adopt it in the 1870's, when he wrote this, because there was then no elaborate scheme of classification, with which books could be closely classified and individualised. Now such schemes of classification are available. Therefore, the world trend is now towards the classified catalogue. The British National Bibliography and the Indian National Bibliography have adopted this type of catalogue. It is too late in the day to go back to the dictionary catalogue or for any new library to adopt that type of catalogue. We have been told of the fox that lost its tail. There are such fox-like librarians who persist in recommending the dictionary catalogue to the libraries being newly formed in India. They are to be pitied; their advice is not to be followed.

Catalogue Code

A catalogue is full of details. There are many alternative

choices possible in respect of many of these details. To catalogue with the aid of a badly drafted or patchy catalogue code will soon make the catalogue a hotch-potch. The only safeguard against this is to adopt a rigorously drafted catalogue code. The only complete and rigorous code for classified catalogue existing today is the Classified Catalogue Code. The other code in vogue is the ALA code. It has no rules for subject entries. It has rules only for author and title entries. Moreover 9 of its rules are faulty and 37 rules are redundant [91]. This has now been realised by its promoters. It is therefore undergoing drastic revision. Further, it is not of much help in rendering Indian names. On the other hand, the Classified Catalogue Code gives useful instructions on this subject. According to Sayers, it is "by far the largest contribution on the subject" [92]. Speaking about it, an American cataloguer says "Of particular interest... are the sections dealing with the structure and rendering of personal names, particularly those of South and South East Asia" [93]. Thus on grounds of merit, the adoption of the Classified Catalogue Code is recommended. Its being of Indian origin is a secondary reason for its adoption.

STRUCTURE OF ENTRIES

Terminology

This chapter deals with the structure of an entry in a card, according to the Classified Catalogue Code. The following terms will be of use in what follows:

Kinds of Entries

1. *Entry.* Ultimate unit-record in a catalogue.

11. *Specific Entry.* Entry mentioning a specific book.

12. *General Entry.* Entry not mentioning any specific book.

13. *Consolidated Entry.* Two or more entries consolidated into a single entry.

14. *Number Entry.* Entry beginning with a call number or a class number.
15. *Word Entry.* Entry beginning with a word, or in rare cases, with a symbol given in the author statement of a document as a substitute for name of author.
16. *Main Entry.* Specific entry giving maximum information about the whole of the book catalogued. All the other entries — specific or general — relating to the document, are normally derived from the main entry.
17. *Added Entry.* Entry other than main entry.

Section of an Entry

18. *Section of an Entry.* That which is prescribed to be a separate paragraph in an entry in a card catalogue.
19. *Leading Section.* Section I of an entry.
20. *Heading Section.*
    1. Leading Section of a word entry.
    2. Section 2 of a call number entry of a book, or of a class number entry of a periodical publication — i e of a main Entry in a classified catalogue.
    3. Section 3 of a *see also* subject entry.
    4. Section 3 of a cross reference index entry.
21. *Tide Section.* Section of a main entry, giving the title of the document catalogued, along with the names of collaborators and of edition if any.
22. *Locus Section.* Section giving the locus in a cross reference entry of a classified catalogue.
23. *Note Section.* Section of a main entry giving the name of the series, if any, to which the book belongs.

24. *Accession Number Section.* Last section in a main entry, giving the accession number of the book.
25. *Tracing Section.* Back of a main entry card, denoting all the added entries of the book.
26. *Second .Section.* Section in a book index entry giving the specification of the concerned book(s).
27. *Directing Section.* Section in an added entry directing attention to a book, or a class number, or an alternative name.
28. *Index Number Section.*
    1. Section in a book index entry, giving the call number of the book.
    2. Section in a class index entry, giving the class number of the class.

Main Entry

Call number entry. Specific subject entry. Subject entry. Specific entry.

22	*Leading Section*	Y733:825 N59
	Heading	Schmidt (Gustav) (1905).
	Title section	How gypsies drink, a descriptive account of their drinking vessels, *tr* by Krishna Pillai Gopala Pillai, from ed 3 of the German. Ed 2.
	Note section	(Indian anthropological series, ed by Kumbakonam Krishna Ayyar, 12).
	Accession number section	135,793.

Cross Reference Entry

Class number entry. Subject analytical. Specific subject entry. Subject entry. Specific entry. Added entry.

23 *Leading section* Y7vl.N5

Directing section *See also* Y738:825 N59

Location section Schmidt.

How gypsies drink, *tr* by Gopala Pillai, ed 2, pp. 250-300.

The class number in the leading section represents "History of the study of ethnology in the world brought up to 1950's."

Author Entry

Specific entry. Added entry.

24 *Heading* Schmidt (Gustav) (1958)

Second section How gypsies drink.

Index number section Y738:S25N59

Translator Entry

Collaboratory entry. Specific entry. Added entry.

25 *Heading* Gopala Pillai (Krishna Pillai) (1912), *tr.*

Second section Schmidt: How gypsies drink.

Index number section Y738:325 N59

Series Entry

Specific entry. Added entry.

26	*Heading*	Indian Anthropological Series.
	Second section	12 Schmidt: How gypsies drink, tr by Gopala Pillai, ed 2.
	Index number section	Y733:825N59

Editor of Series Entry

Cross reference index entry. General entry.

27	Referred *from heading*	Krishna Ayyar (Kumbekonam) (1892), Ed.
	Directing section	*See also*
	Referred to heading	Indian Anthropological Series.

Class Index Entry

Subject entry. General entry.

28	*Heading*	Drinking Vessel.
	Directing section	For books in this class and its subclasses see the Classified Part of this catalogue under the Class Number
	Index number section	Y738:825

Library Hand

Writing should be in detached upright impersonal hand. This is called Library Hand. This is necessary because, with each one writing in his own hand, not conforming to this standard, will make the catalogue ugly. For, the catalogue cards will be written by successive cataloguers. But all the cards will be kept together permanently.

Style of Writing

Similarly it is necessary to conform to one fixed standard in respect of space between words, space between class number and book number, formation of paragraphs, indention of paragraphs, and writing of numbers other than call number. To facilitate this, the standard catalogue card is 125 x 75 mm. It is ruled horizontally to take the writing. It has two vertical rules — the first vertical at a distance of 10 mm from the left shorter edge and the second vertical at a further distance of 5 mm from the first. The following items are to begin at the vertical:

1. Leading section;
2. Heading of every kind;
3. Continuation lines of all sections; and
4. Accession number section.

Any section, other than the index number section and those specified for the first vertical, is to be given at the second vertical. The index number section is to be written in the line in which the title section or the series section, as the case may be, ends if there is sufficient space in it. It is to begin as far to the right as possible in its line, so as to end just near the end of that line.

Capitals, Italics, and Numerals

All the letters, except those of a conjunction if any, in any heading of any kind are to be in capitals. The first letter after a colon is to be in capital. Otherwise, the usual convention of prose is to be followed. The title portion in any entry is to be written as if it were a sentence in prose — that is, no word in the title except the first is to be begun with a capital letter, unless it is a proper noun. A descriptive term, such as *EJ, Tr, Comm,* occurring in a heading, is to begin with a capital notwithstanding its following a comma. The term is to be underlined. In print, it will be in italics. All numbers other than class number and book number are to be written in Indo-Arabic numerals. The following collection symbols may be used:

1. Pamphlet. Underline book number.
2. Over-sized book. Overline book number.
3. Book of poor build; such as a book with many plates. Underline and overline book number.
4. Book to be kept in the reading room for ready reference. Add "R R" above the Class Number.
5. Book to be kept temporarily in the topical collection. Put in the first vacant line of its date-label the date fixed for its release from the topical sequence and encircle it.

Punctuation Mark

Punctuation marks are to be as in ordinary prose, subject to the following modifications:

1. A comma is to separate two consecutive blocks in the heading. See examples 11 to 15 in section 8161, 19 to 21 in section 8162, 1-7 in section 8332.
2. A comma is to separate a Descriptive Element in a block in a heading from what it separates. See examples 25 of section " 8221 and 27 of 8241.
3. Circular brackets are to enclose each individualising

secondary element in a block in a heading or the heading as a whole, as the case may be. See examples 1, 2 and 4 of section 811, 5 of section 8141, 8 of section 8153, 10 of section 8156, 22 of section 821, 24 of section 822, 25 of section 8221, and 27 of 8241.

Arrangement of Entries

Classified Part

The entries in the classified part of the catalogue are to be arranged by their respective class numbers. Of the entries with the same class number, those with book numbers are to precede those without book numbers. The former are to be arranged by their respective book numbers. The latter are to be arranged among themselves by the book numbers in the third section and the words in the fourth section.

Alphabetical Part

The entries in the alphabetical part of the catalogue are to be arranged alphabetically as in a dictionary. There are some conventions to be followed. Only the letters actually written in the entry are to be taken into consideration. That is, contractions are not to be arranged as if they were expanded. In particular, as an example, Scotch names beginning with "Mac" should come together. Those beginning with "Mc" should come together in their own place. Again, "New York" is to precede "Newark". This is called "Nothing before something" rule. For more complicated cases, the original Classified Catalogue Code should be consulted.

RENDERING OF NAME IN HEADING

Introduction

The following is a list of the kind of names likely to occur in headings of entries. The later sections of this chapter indicate the way of rendering them in the headings:

1. Name-of-person;
2. Geographical name;
3. Name of government;
4. Name of institution;
5. Name of conference;
6. Name of book — that is, title; and
7. Name of series — that is, publisher's series.

Here the following definitions will be of use:

1. **Entry Element.** The word or word group prescribed to be written first in a heading, main heading, or subheading.
2. **Entry Word.** The first word of an entry element.
3. **Secondary Element.** The word or word group occurring in a name but not selected as entry element and therefore to be written after it.

A secondary element has the status of an individualising element. Further, while taking a name-of-person from the title-page any word denoting academic degree, civil or military honours, and all honorific words are to be ignored. The words left over in the name-of-person may be called the *Reduced Name.*

Name-of-Person

Simple Name

An oversimplified rule is "Make the last word in a name-of-person the entry word. Make all the other words the secondary element." This will work well in:

1. Most modern names of the West;
2. A modern name of Assam, Bengal, Gujarat, Kashmir, Maharashtra, Orissa, and Sindh; and

3. A modern name of South India, not ending with an attached word — such as Ayyangar, Ayyar, Chettiar, Mudaliar, Pillai, etc — indicating sub-community. In the first two cases, the last word denotes *Family Name;* and the earlier words denote *Given Names* —- that is, name or names given during the naming ceremony or later. In Marathi and Gujarati, one of the earlier words is father's given name. In the third case, the last words denote the Given Name; the earlier words may denote father's name, or family name, or name of locality.

In a South Indian name with an attached word, such as those indicated in section 8311 —the entry element is to consist of the word group made of the Given Name preceding the attached word followed by the attached word itself. The other words from the secondary element. For example, see examples 25 of section 8221 and 27 of section 8241.

In the Hindi and Punjabi name-of-person not having a family name in imitation of the West, the original single coalesced *(Samasa)* word denoting the given name is split into two or more words. All the components of the split word should be taken together as a word-group for use as entry element. For example, *Labhu Ram, Manohar Lal,* and *Rama Prasad.*

Complicated Cases

The original Classified Catalogue Code should be used for complicated cases with double and treble family names, whose whole word-group should be used as entry element. So also, for Muslim names and for lists of irremovable attachment at the end of South Indian names.

Reduction of Homonym

Historically, the secondary element was used, in a heading made of a name-of-person, chiefly to resolve homonyms. In spite of it, homonyms may crop up. Such homonyms are to be resolved by adding the year of birth of the person as a further individualising element. It should be enclosed in a circular bracket. It is now considered desirable to add the year of birth in all possible cases to avoid the formation of homonyms in future.

Geographical Name

The name of a geographical entity is to be written in the favoured language of the library, if it has a name in that language. It is to be written in the language of its own locality, if it does not have a name in the favoured language of the library.

Homonym: Areas Outside One Another

If two or more geographical areas have the same name and lie in different countries, the individualising element for resolving the homonym is to be the name of the country in which it lies, except that it may be omitted if it is the country of the library. If two or more geographical areas have the same name and lie outside one another, the individualising element for resolving the homonym is to be the name of the largest geographical area, among the areas of the countries, constituent states, districts, taluks, etc containing that the respective geographical areas and sufficient to individualise them.

Homonym: Area Within Area

If two or more geographical areas have the same name and lie one within another in succession, the individualising element for resolving the homonym is to be the word state, district, taluk, city, town, village, etc, as the case may be, except that it can be omitted if it is the name of the largest of the above mentioned areas among those needed for resolving the homonym.

Name of Government

Definition

The term "Government" is used to denote a corporate body with,

1. Full sovereign power, as the Government of India, or Government of Britain, or Government of USA;
2. Limited sovereign power as the Governments of the States of M.P., Bihar, or New York;
3. Without sovereign power, but a local body established for the regulation, promotion, and/or provision of specific public services in an area, such as Bhopal District Board, Bhopal Taluk Board, or Bhopal City Municipality; and
4. Any constitutional or administratively created organ of any of the above.

Name of Whole Government

When used as the corporate author of a book, the name of the government is to be the name of its territory.

Examples

1. India is the rendering of "Government of India".
2. Madhya Pradesh is the rendering of the "Government of the constituent state Madhya Pradesh ".
3. Bhopal (District) is the rendering of the "District Board of Bhopal District".

4. Bhopal (Taluk) is the rendering of the "Local Body or the Taluk Board of the Bhopal Taluk".
5. Bhopal (City) is the rendering of the "Local Body or the Municipal Council of the City of Bhopal ".

Constitutional Organ

In the case of an organ of a government, the first heading is to be the name of the whole government. Then should come the name of the organ as subheading:

Examples

1. India, president.
2. India, cabinet.
3. India, lok sabha.
4. India, supreme court.
5. Allahabad, high court.
6. Allahabad (City), mayor.
7. Allahabad (City), council.

Administrative Departments of Government

In the case of an administrative department of a government, the first heading is to be the name of the whole government. Then should come the name of the department as subheading. In the subheading, the word or word group denoting the sphere of work is to be the entry element. It should be reduced to the noun form in the nominative case. The other words in the name of the department are to be made a secondary element, and added within circular brackets. The place of the entry element should be indicated by a dash within the brackets cantaining the secondary clement.

Example

1. India, Finance (Ministry of —).

2. Tamil Nadu, Instruction (Department of Public —).
3. Maharashtra, Agriculture (—Department). Assuming that it is called Agricultural Department.

Temporary Organ

In the case of a temporary organ of a government, the year of its formation is to be added as an individualising element.

Examples

1. India, Banking (Indian Central — Enquiry Committee) (1929).
2. West Bengal, Public Libraries (Review Committee on—)(1960).
3. West Bengal, Legislative Assembly, Public Libraries Bill (Select Committee on —) (1948).

Name of Institution

Definition

The term "Institution" is used to denote an independent or autonomous corporate body, other than a government, whether:

1. created by a government;
2. constituted under a statute; or
3. formed voluntarily — formally or informally. The term denotes also an Organ of an Institution.

Name of Whole Institution

The name to be used in rendering the name of an institution is to be the one in the shortest form found in the:

1. tide-page; or

2. half-title page; or
3. any other part of the book.

The initial article and every honorific word not forming an inseparable part of the name, if any, are to be omitted. Whenever necessary, individualising element is to be added.

Examples

1. Andhra University.
2. Asiatic Society of Bengal, and Not Royal Asiatic Society of Bengal.
3. Royal Society of London, as the Word "Royal" is inseparable from the name.
4. Srinivasa Sastry Entertainment Committee, and not Rt. Honorable Srinivasa Sastry Entertainment Committee.
5. State Bank of India (Delhi).
6. State Bank of India (Madras) (City).
7. University Grants Commission (India).

Name of Organ of Institution

In the case of an organ of an institution, the first heading is to be the name of the whole institution. Then should come the name of the organ as subheading. The latter should be rendered as in the case of an organ of the government.

Name of a Conference

Definition

The term "Conference" is used to denote a meeting for deliberation, or formulation or expression of opinion or sentiment,

1. not convened by government(s) and made up of its (their) own personnel;
2. not convened by and made up only of the members of a single institution or to form an institution; but
3. convened and conducted either spontaneously by a number of persons or institutions to consider matters of common interest; or
4. convened by a body with no function or existence beyond the conference convened and held by it. The term denotes also an Organ of a Conference.

Individualisation

The rendering of the name of a conference is to be on the analogy of that for institution. And the name of the place or/ and the year of the conference is/are to be added as individualising element(s).

Example

1. Basant Memorial Meeting (1933).
2. Conference of Orientalists (Simla) (1911).
3. Geneva Summit Conference (1956).

Title of a Book

Initial Article and Honorific

The initial article and honorific, if any, are to be omitted in rendering the title of the book either in a heading or in any other section.

Puff

Puff, if any, in the title of a book is to be omitted. In the main entry, in the title section, its place should be indicated by "... ". In an added entry, in the second section, such an indication is not necessary; the title may be used in a shortened form, without taking away intelligibility.

In the Heading

When the title occurs in a heading, the first two words are to be deemed to form the entry element.

Name of Series

In rendering the name of the series, in the note section or in the heading, the initial article and honorific words, if any, are to be omitted. And the remaining words are to be written in the sequence in which they occur in the book. If the name of the series is not an individualising one — for example, English series. Publication series, Translation series — its name is to be preceded by the name of an individualising entity with which it is associated, say as publisher, sponsor, university. The name of the entity used as the individualising entity is to be rendered as prescribed for the entities of its kind.

The style of writing will be as shown above in the note section of the main entry. If the name of the series occurs in the heading of an entry, caps and small caps will be used in the usual style.

Who is the Author?

The name of the author is to be taken from the title-page. It is usually indicated there. If it is not indicated, the book is to be taken to be anonymous. For most of the books, the author is a single person. For some, it may be two or more persons. In both these cases, it is a person or persons, who create the thought content of the book and express it. Such a book of personal authorship will give no difficulty, unless there are collaborators. Some books are produced on the responsibility of a corporate body — a government, an institution, or a conference — or two or more corporate bodies. They are responsible for the thought content and for the expression. Such a book is of corporate authorship. Some difficulty may arise in books of this kind. The difficulty arises when the title-page of a book of corporate authorship gives the name of a person also. The following sections give a summary of the convention used to solve such difficulties. For a full discussion of the problem.

Person *vs* Person

Ser Numb	*Type of Work*	*Author*
1.	Ana. table-talk	Talker
2.	Dialogue, conversation, debate	Participants
3.	Interview	Person(s) interviewed
4.	Narration (real and not fictitious)	Narrator
5.	Mediumistic communication	Medium(s) and not the disembodied soul(s)
6.	Correspondence	Correspondent(s) unless it is all of one person only with several others in which case only that one person

Dependent Work or Kind

The author of the original work should be taken as the author of the following kinds of dependent works. The other associated person is to be taken, only as collaborator:

1. Abridgment
2. Adaptation
3. Paraphrase
4. Revision
5. Selection
6. Translation

Dependent Work of Kind 2

The author of the dependent work itself should be taken as the author of the following kinds of dependent work:

1. Commentary	91 Novelisation
2. Concordance	92 Parody
3. Continuation	93 Sequel
4. Dramatisation	94 Supplement
5. Imitation	95 Versification
6. Index	96 Version in the same or another
7. Libretto	language, which has sufficient
8. Music-setting	new qualities in thought and/or expression to deem it an independent work on its own right.

Person *vs* Corporate Body

If the title-page mentions the name(s) of person(s) only and does not mention or indicate the name of any corporate body other than the one belonging to the publishing trade mentioned in the imprint, the work is of personal authorship.

If the title-page does not mention the name of any person but mentions or indicates the name of a corporate body other than a body belonging to the publishing trade mentioned in the imprint, the work is of corporate authorship.

Even if the title page mentions a person, if it indicates the name of a corporate body other than the publisher, the work is of corporate authorship, if it is of a deliberative, legislative, directive, judicial, administrative, or routine character limited by the purpose or function or outlook of the corporate body. But the mere fact that the book is published, financed, aided, approved, sponsored, or authorised by a corporate body is not sufficient reason to deem it to be of corporate authorship.

On the other hand, if the primary purpose of the book is the extension of the boundary of the field of knowledge, or its intensification, and the responsibility for the thought-content and expression of it, rests on the person and not on the office held by him in the corporate body, it is of personal authorship. The mere mention of the personal name of an official of the corporate body in the title-page is not sufficient reason to deem it to be of personal authorship.

Government *vs* Institution

Group 1

Each of the following institutions is to be taken as author of its works, as if it were independent of the parent body, if any exists, be it government or institution:

Abbey	Exchange (Money)	Post office
Bank		Produce exchange
Board of Trade	Firm of Enterprise	Religious order
Cathedral	Foundation	School
Cemetery	Guild	Stock-exchange
Chamber of Commerce	Masonic body	Telegraph office
Church (place of worship)	Monastery	Telephone exchange
College	Mosque	Temple
Convent	Park	University
Endowment	Political party	

Group 2

Each of the following institutions are to be taken as author of its work as if it were independent of the parent body, provided it has a distinctive name:

Botanical garden	Hospital	Museum
Chapel	Laboratory	Observatory
Experimental station	Library	Zoological garden
Exhibition		

Note: If any of the above institutions has no distinctive name, it should be treated as an organ of its parent body.

Group 3

Any formal or informal group of the members of a parent body, formed for recreative, ameliorative, or any other economical or social purposes other than forming a distinctive purpose of the parent body, should be treated as an organ of the parent body, even if it has a distinctive name.

HEADING OF MAIN ENTRY

Introduction

The structure — that is the sections, their sequence, and their make-up — have been shown by examples in section 821. The rendering of the heading and of the later sections. This chapter deals only with the choice of heading for the main entry of the book.

Choice of Heading

The heading is to consist of the earliest of the following, which the book admits:

1. The name of personal author;
2. The names of joint personal authors;
3. The name of corporate author;
4. The names of joint corporate authors;
5. Pseudonym;
6. The name of collaborator;
7. The names of joint collaborators; and
8. The title of the book.

Two Joint Authors

If the title-page contains the names of two and only two joint authors, both the names are to be used as the heading with the conjunction "and" connecting them.

Example

1. Srinivasan (G A) (1894) and Krishnamachari (C) (1894).
2. American Library Association and Library Association (UK).
3. Indian Standards Institution, Documentation (—Section) and Insdoc, Technical (—Committee).

Three or More Joint Authors

If the title-page contains the names of three or more joint authors, the name of the first mentioned author alone is to be used as the heading and the word "etc" is to be added thereafter.

Example

Ranganathan (Shiyali Ramamrita) (1892) etc. is the heading for the *Union catalogue of learned periodicals of South Asia* (1953) which has 20 other joint authors.

Pseudonym

A pseudonym is a false or fictitious name used by an author in the title-page of the book. If the title-page gives only a pseudonym, the pseudonym is to be used as the heading and it is to be followed by the descriptive element *"Pseud"*. If the title-page gives the real name of the author also in a subordinated manner, it is to be added in circular brackets after the descriptive element. The real name is to be preceded by the symbol "i *e*". A comma is to be placed before the bracket begins.

Example

Libra, *Pseud.*

Twain (Mark), *Pseud.*

Twain (Mark), *Pseud, (i e* Samuel Langhore Clement).

Collaborator Heading

If the title-page does not give the name of personal author(s) or indicate corporate authorship or give a pseudonym, but contains the name of collaborator, that name is to be used as the heading; and a descriptive element is to be added thereafter indicating the role of the collaborator.

Title-Heading

If a book is a general biographical dictionary or an encyclopaedia belonging to the class generalia, or science general, or useful arts, or social sciences, or is a volume of a periodical, or if the heading cannot be Chosen in accordance with the prescriptions in sections 851 to 855, the title, is to be used as the heading.

HEADING OF BOOK INDEX ENTRY

The structure — that is section(s) etc — of a book index entry has been shown by examples in sections 822, 8221 and 824. The rendering of the heading and of the later sections. This chapter deals only with the choice of the headings for which book index entries are to be given for a book.

A book index entry is to be given using as heading each of such of the following, as the main entry of the book admits of.

1. Derived from Heading

1. Heading, provided it is not, as such, eligible to be used as the heading of a class index entry appropriate to the book;
2. Each permutation of the names in the heading, if it is one of two joint authors or two collaborators;
3. Name of each of the third and later authors, if there are three or more joint authors (optional).

Derived from Title Section

1. Name of each collaborator mentioned in the Title portion; and
2. Title of the book,
    1. If it is fanciful; or
    2. If it contains a proper noun; or
    3. If it is treated in usage as a proper noun, provided that it is not, as such, eligible to be used as the heading of a class index entry of the book.

Derived from Note Section

Name of the series occurring in each independent series note.

HEADING OF CROSS REFERENCE INDEX ENTRY

The structure — that is the section(s) etc — of a cross reference index entry has been shown by examples in section 8241. The rendering of the referred-from-heading has been described in Chapter 83. The referred-to-heading is to be the same as in the main entry or book index entry to which it relates. This chapter deals only with the types of cross reference index entry.

A cross reference index entry may be one of the four types:

1. Alternative name entry;
2. Variant-form-of-word entry;
3. Pseudonym-real-name entry; and
4. Editor-of-series entry.

Care is to be taken not to write a cross reference index entry suggested by a book, if an identically similar entry is already found in the catalogue.

Alternative Name Entry

There is to be an alternative name entry using as referred-from-heading each of all the possible alternative names by which any person, any corporate body, any geographical entity, any series, or any book, respectively whose name has been used as the heading of the main entry or a book index entry, is known or is likely to be known.

Variant-Form-of-Word Entry

There is to be a variant-form-of-word entry using as referred-from-heading each of all possible variant forms in which the word(s) in the name of a person or a corporate body or a geographical entity or a book, occurring in the heading of a main entry or a book index entry, or an alternative name index entry, has(have) occurred or is(are) likely to occur.

Pseudonym-real-name Entry

There is to be a pseudonym-real-name entry in the case of every person whose pseudonym alone or pseudonym as well as real name appears in the main entry concerned. The referred-to-heading is to be the pseudonym.

Editor-of-series Entry

There is to be an editor-of-series entry using as referred-from-heading the name(s) of the editor(s), if any, occurring in the series note in any main entry in the catalogue. In the case of joint editors, an editor-of-series entry is to be made for each of the permuted sequences of the names. The referred-to-heading is to be name of the series.

HEADING OF CLASS INDEX ENTRY

The sections of index entry have been shown by illustration in section 825. The choice and rendering of the headings of class index entries is regulated by the Chain Procedure. It is a method using the class number of the book for the purpose. It is illustrated here by throwing into a chain the class number of the book whose main entry is given as example 22 in section 821. For every book, the class index heading should also be derived from the class numbers in all its cross references entries. Care should be taken that the same cross reference entry is not made in the catalogue more than once.

Chain for the Class Number in Example 22

Y	=	Sociology
	↓	sought heading)
Y7	=	Ethnology
	↓	(Sought heading)
Y73	=	Ethnic groups
	↓	(Sought heading)
Y738	=	Gypsy
	↓	(Sought heading)
Y738:3	=	Equipment of gypsies
	↓	(Sought heading)
Y738:32	=	Utensils of gypsies
	↓	(Sougth heading)
Y738:325	=	Drinking vessels of gypsies
	↓	(Sought heading)

Chain for the Class Number in Example 23

Y	=	Sociology
	↓	(sought heading) (But already written)
Y7	=	Ethnology
	↓	(Sought heading) (But already written)

Y7v	=	History of Ethnology
	↓	(Sought heading)
Y7vl	=	History of ethnology in the world
	↓	(Sought heading)
Y7vI.N5	=	History of ethnology in the world brought up to 1950's
	↓	(Unsought heading)

MAIN LIBRARY TERMS

Accession

— number

Act

Adaptation

Adaptor

Added entry

Additional

Administration

Alphabetical sequence

Alphabetisation

Alternative

— title

Arrangement

Array

Artificial composite book

Assistant

Author

Author-analytical

Author-catalogue

Charged tray
Charging
— tray
Chronological sequence
Circulation
City central library
Class
— index entry
— number
Classic
Classification
Classificationist
Classified catalogue
— sequence
Classifier
Code
Co-extensiveness
Collaborator
Collection
Collection symbol
College library
Colon
— Classification
Colophon
Commentator
Compilation
Compiler
Composite book

Editing
Edition
Editor
Encyclopaedia
Entrance
Entry (Catalogue)
Epitomizer
Evolutionary sequence
Extract
Exchange list
Exit
Facet
Facet-formula
Fascicule
Filiation
Filiatory
— sequence
First vertical
Five Laws of Library Science
Focus
Formula
Function
Fundamental
— constituent term
Furniture
Gangway guide
Generalia class
Gate register

Geographical facet
— sequence
Guarantee
Guarantor
Guide
— card
Half-title
Heading
Helpful sequence
Horizontal line
Impression
Imprint
Inclusive notation
Index
— entry
Initionym
Issue
— (of periodicals)
— counter
Job
— Immediate
Joint author
— editor
Later title
Leading line
— section
Librarian
Library

— hand

Loan

Long-range reference

Main class

— entry

Maintenance section

Member

Membership card

Multi-faceted

Multifocal

Multivolumed

National Central Library

Notation

Note

Number

— (of a periodical)

Octave principle

Off-print

Open access

— notation

Ordering

Ordinal number

Ordinary composite book

Organisation

Overdue

Pamphlet

Parallel movement

Parody

Reprinted
Research library
Reserved collection
Return
— counter
— date
Reviser
Room
Routine
Rule
Rural central library
Scheme
School library
Second vertical
Serial
— number
Series
— note
Set
Schedule
Shelf
— arrangement
— guide
— register
— section
— work
Short title
Simple book

Three-phased

Tier guide

Title

Title-page

— Back of the

Train

Translator

Travelling library

Tray

Two-phased

Unifocal

Unipartite

University library

Vendor

Verso

Vertical file

Volume

Who's who

Wicket gate

Work

REFERENCES

Kabir, Abulfazal M. "Ranganathan: A Universal Librarian." *Journal of Educational Media and Library Sciences*. 40:4 (June 2003) :453-59.

Ranganathan, Shiyali Ramamrita. *The Five Laws of Library Science*. London: Edward Goldston. 1931.

Ranganathan, Shiyali Ramamrita. "The Five Laws of Library and information Science", Delhi, Ess Ess Publications (Reprint) 2007.

Rubin, Richard E. *Foundations of Library and Information Science*. 2nd ed. New York: Neal-Schuman Publishers. 2004.

Glossary

AACR2: *Anglo-American Cataloging Rules, 2nd ed., revised.* (American Library Association, the Library Association (U.K.) and the Canadian Library Association, 1988-). A detailed set of standardized rules for cataloging various types of library materials. Divided into two parts: rules for creting the bibliogrpahic description and rules governing the choice and form of entry of headings (access points) in the catalog.

AMIM I: *Archival Moving Image Materials: a Cataloging Manual,* 1st ed. (Library of Congress, 1984). Superceded by AMIM II. Rules for describing archival moving image materials. Intended to provide guidance within the general framework of the *Anglo-American Catalogiuing Rules,* 2nd edition (AACR2)

APPM: *Archives, Personal Papers, and Manuscripts: a Cataloging Manual for Archival Repositories, Historical Societies and Manuscript Libraries.* 2nd ed. (Society of American Archivists, 1989). Rules for describing primarily textual archival collections, although it includes rules for moving images. Intended to provide guidance within the general framework of the *Anglo-American Catalogiuing Rules,* 2nd edition (AACR2).

Audience: Constituencies or clientele served by the moving image organization.

Catalog: A formal inventory, description, and locating aid to the holdings of an archive, library, museum or other repository, often in card form or computer database form,

Card: A paper card, usually 3 x 5 inches in dimension, upon which a catalog record is typed or printed, after which the card is filed in a drawer, in some order, usually alphabetical.

Cataloging level: Refers to the level of focus for a cataloing record or description—higher than, lower than, or at te title level (resource level).

Classification scheme: A scheme, usually consisting of numbers or alphanumericor other notation that categorizes or subdivides a subject area or collection of materials. Most classification schemes were originally intended to organize physical items on the shelf. The result was a unique shelving location (call number) for each item that facilitated browsing of material by subject or author.

Collection level: Refers to a cataloging description or record that focuses on a collection or grouping of moving image or audio resources without necessarily describing or fully cataloging the individual resources.

Complementary resources: Non-moving image resources which complement or support the organization's moving image collection.

Content standard: A detailed set of rules for preparing bibliographic records to describe and represent items added to a library or archival collection. A content standard is established to maintain consistency within the catalog and between the catalogs or libraries or archives using the same standard. the word 'content' refers tp tje content of the bibliographic or descriptive record, not the content of the resource being described, such as a moving image resource.

DDC: *Dewey Decimal Classification:* http: //www.oclc.org/dewey. A system of classifying library and archival materials, particularly in small and medium size libraries. An all-numeric systems, with new numbers added by decimal expansion.

Dublin Core: *Dublin Core Metadata Element Set* (Dublin Core Metadata Initiative): http: //dublincore.org/. A standard set of 15 elements (title, creator, subject, etc.), with optional qualifiers and community-specific extensions. All elements are optional and repeatable within an application profile used to structure data elements into records customized for specific audiences. Dublin Core is used to structure descriptive information about a resource but also to map readily to other descriptive schema, to facilitate sharing information across different metadata schemas and user communities. First developed in the mid-1990s, and originally intended for use in describing web sites and web pages, Dublin Core is now used also for describing physical and digital collections in museums, libraries, archives and other repositories.

EAD: *Encoded Archival Description* (Society of American Archivisits, maintained by the Library of Congress): http: //lcweb.loc.gov/ead. A data intrechange standard that defines the structural elements (and their interrelationships) to be used in creating archival inventories or registers (finding aids that supplement broad collection descriptions for archival collections). *EAD* includes descriptive metadata, metadata about the owning archive and the provenance of the material being described, in addition to the structural finding aid.

FIAF: The *FIAF Cataloguing Rules for Film Archives* (Fédération

Internationale des Archives du Film - K.G. Saur, 1991). ryles for describing archival moving image materials, developed for an international audience by FIAF (Fédération Internationale des Archives du Film, or International Federation of Film Archives). Out of print.

Finding aids: Guides, inventories, indexes, registers, lists, or other sstems for retrieving archival materials. Finding aids usually provide detailed listings of individual items described collectively in a "collection-level" or "series-level" record. Typically used in archival collections, particularly text-based collections, for primary source materials, where full cataloging at the item level is cost-prohibitive.

IEEE-LOM: *Institute of Electrical and Electronics Engineers (IEEE)-Learning Object Metadata* (IEEE): http: //ltsc.ieee.org/wg12/. IEEE standard 1484.12.1 -2002, a set of data elements used to structure descriptive records and facilitate information sharing among learning communities. Intended for use in describing learning objects, online learning or instructional materials which have been created by a variety of learning software products, such as learning management systems, presentation software or complex authoring software. Developed in the late 1990s.

In-house: Any system, scheme or practice developed by and for a local archive, library, museum or other repository, and generally used only by that repository.

ISBD: *International Standard Bibliographic Description* (International Federation of Library Associations (IFLA)): http: //www.ifla.org/VII/s13/pubs/isbdg.htm. Bibliographic standard providing a general framework for the description of different kinds of library materials (books, serials, electronic resources, etc.), including the order of elements in the catalog entry and prescribed punctuation. ISBDs have been integrated into sevearl catalog codes around the world, including the *Anglo-American Cataloguing Rules, 2nd ed. (AACR2) and Archival Moving Image Materials: a Cataloging Manual (AMIM).*

LCC: *Library of Congress Classification* (Library of Congress): http: //www.loc.gov/catdir/cpso/lcco.html. A system of classifying library and archival materials, particularly in larger research collections. Divides human knowledge into 20 broad categories indicated by single letters of the roman alphabet, with major subdivisions indicated by a second letter, and narrower subdivisions by decimal numbers and further alphabetic notation.

LCNAF: *Library of Congress Name Authority File* (Library of Congress). A comprehensive controlled vocabularly (established list of preferred terms, often with cross references), primarily of names and jurisdictions, used by thousands of institutions to describe and index persons or bodies who are the subject, or are responsible for the intellectual content of, library and archival material. Part of the *Library of Congress Authorities* (http: //authorities.loc.gov/)

LCSH: *Library of Congress Subject Headings* (Library of Congress). A comprehensive controlled vocabulary (established list of preferred terms, often with cross references), primarily of topical subjects, with cross references, broader terms, narrower terms, and scope notes. *LCSH* is used by thousands of institutions to describe and index the content or subject of library and archival material. Developed for print material but also used for moving images. Part of the *Library of Congress Authorities* (http: //authorities.loc.gov/)

MARC: *MAchine Readable Cataloging* (Library of Congress): http: //www.loc.gov/marc/marc.html. A series of detailed standards for the structuring or tagging of data to facilitate the interchange of records between databases or files. The principal format is teh *MARC 21 Format for Bibliographic Data,* used for descriptions of library and archival materials. There are also formats for *Authority* (for controlled vocabularies, or established lists of preferred terms with cross references, *Holdings, Classification,* and *Community Information.* First developed in the 1960s.

MeSH: *MEdical Subject Headings* (National Library of Medicine, U.S.): http: //www.nlm.nih.giv/mesh/meshhome.html. A comprehensive controlled vocabulary (established list of preferred terms, often with cross references), primarily of topical subjects, with cross references, broader terms, narrower terms, and scope notes, used to describe and index the content or subject of library and archival materials in the field of medicine.

Metadata schema: A labeling, tagging or coding system used for recording cataloging information or structuring descriptive records. A metadata schema establishes and defines data elements and the rules governing the use of data elements to describe a resource.

Microform: A storage medium for stroing printed text or images in photographically reduced size on a fil, usually in the form of a microfilm roll or microfiche card.

MODS: *Metadata Object Description Schema* (Library of Congress): http: //www.loc.gov/standards/mods. A standard set of elements or labels to structure descriptive records in XML (eXtensible Markup Language). Intended to be able to carry selected data from existing *MARC 21* records, as well as to enable to creation of original descriptive records. It includes a subset of *MARC 21* bibliographic fields and uses language-based tags rather than numeric ones, in some cases regrouping elements from the *MARC 21* bibliogrpahic format. Defined as an XML schema (http: //www.w3.org/XML/Schema) of the World Wide Web Consortium (http: //www.w3.org/).

MPEG-7: *MPEG-7,* formally known as *Multimedia Content Description Interface* or ISO 15938 (Motion Picture Experts Group): http: //mpeg.telecomitalialab.com/ standards/mpeg-7/mpeg-7.htm. A set of standardized tools to describe multimedia resources, including still images, mocing images, audio, etc. Includes textual and nontextual indexing and description. Defined as an XML schema (http: //www.w3.org/XML/Schema) of the World Wide Web Consortium (http: // www.w3.org/). Expressed in XML (eXtensible Markup Language). Originally released in late 2001.

NLM: *NLM Classification* (National Library of Medicine, U.S.): http: //wwwcf.nlm.nih.gov/class. A system of classifying library and archival materials in the field of medicine and related sciences. Designed for use in both large and small library collections. The NLM Classification is a system of mixed notation patterned after the Library of Congress Classification (LCC).

No catalog: An archive or library with no catalog provides no textual method of structuring and locating moving image resources, such as a database, card catalog, printed catalog or finding aid.

OAI data mining: The collecting or harvesting of cataloging or metadata inforamtion from OAI compliant databases of repositories, archives, libraries, etc., using the Open Archives Initiative Protocol. Service providers request data from data provider archives, often according to date stamps. http: // www.openarchives.org/

Online networked computer (not web-accessible): A computerized catalog that is connected to a local area of wide area netowkr and can be searched by catalog users connected to the same network, but cannot be searched via the Internet and a web browser.

Portal: A website offering a wide variety of resources, services and links, especially one offering services within a particular industry, occupation or field or customizing services to a particular audience.

Print catalog, list or brochure: A repository's catalog that exists in card, book, or printout form, or as a printed list, book, or brochure.

RAD: *Rules for Archival Description* (Association of Canadian Archivists). Rules for describing archival collections in all formats, including moving images, maps, photographs, electronic records, sound recordings and textual materials. Based on the premise that description should occur on multiple levels (collection, series, title, etc.)

RAK: *Regeln in die alphabetische Katalogisierung,* Rules for describing materials in all formats. The German cataloging code, analogous to the *Ango-American Cataloguing Rules, 2nd ed.*

RICA: *Regole Italiane di Catalogazione per Autori* (Commissione permanente per l'aggiornamento della RICA). rules for describing materials in all formats. The Italian cataloging code, analogous to the *Ango-American Cataloguing Rules, 2nd ed.*

Segment level: Refers to a cataloging description or record that focuses on one or more segments in a moving image or audio resource.

Series level: Refers to a cataloging description or record that focuses on the series that the individual moving image or audio resources are part of.

Shot level: Refers to a cataloging description or record that focuses on one or more shorts in a moving image resource.

SMEF: *Standard Media Exchange Framework* (British Broadcasting Corporation): http: //www.bbc.co.uk/guidelines/smef/SMEF. A data dictionary which defines the attributes of data, the entities into which the data is grouped, and the relationships between these entities. It attempts to include all data a business needs to know about a particular media item throughout the lifecycle.

SMPTE: *SMPTE Metadata Dictionaliry with associated guidelines and recommended practices* (Society of Moving Pictures and Television Engineers). Metadata schema for digital audiovisual materials, designed for the production environment and covering the entire production chain: pre-production, post-production, acquisition, distribution, broadcasting, storage and archiving.

Standalone computer: A computer that is not connected to any online network and thus cannot share data with another computer.

SuDocs: *Superintendent of Documents Classification* (Superintendent of Documents, U.S. Government

Printing Office): http: //www.access.gpo.gov/su_docs/fdlp/pubs/explain.html. A system for classifying publications of the U.S. federal government, which is designed to uniquely identify, logically related, and physically arrange each publication so that all publications of a single agency or department may be found together.

Subject heading list: A controlled vocabulary (established list of preferred terms, usually with cross references), generally of topical subjects, which can be added to a descriptive record to enable search and retrieval by subject.

Title level: Refers to a cataloging description or record that focuses on the entire moving image or audio resource.

ULAN: *Union List of Artist Names* (Getty Research Institute): http: //www.getty.edu/research/tools/vocabulary/ulan/ . A structured vocabulary containing names and information about individuals and "corporate bodies" (i.e., groups of people working together in a formal collaboration), involved in the design or creation of art and architecture. Scope is global and covers antiquity to the present. *ULAN* contains about 220,000 names. Entries include spelling variants, nicknames, pseudonyms, biographical data, etc.

Union catalog: A catalog that represents the holdings of more than one repository (archive, library, museum, etc.)

URL: Uniform Resource Locator, the unique address which identifies a resource on the Internet for routing purposes, such as http: //www.filmarchive.org.

VRA Core: *Visual Resources Association Core Categories* (Visual Resources Association): http: //www.vraweb.org/vracore3.htm. A standard set of about 17 elements, with optional qualifiers, used to structure descriptive records and facilitate information sharing, intended for use in describing "works of visual culture," as we;; as the images that document them.

Web-accessible: Refers to a networked, online computerized catalog that can be searched by catalog users over the Internet, using a web browser. Catalog records will display in a format that can be read and displayed by a browser, such as HTML (Hypertext Markup Language) or XML (eXtensible Markup Language)

Z39.50: A standard which specifies a technical protocol for searching and retrieving information from multiple remote online catalogs or other Z39.50-compliant databases, regardless of the native search commands of those individual catalogs or databases. "Z39.50" refers to the numbers of the ISO and ANSI/NISO standards (ISO 23950 and ANSI/NISO Z39.50). The Library of Congress is the maintenance agency and registration authority for both standards, which are technically identical.

BIBLIOGRAPHY

Agarwal, V., 2000. *Library Acquisition and Cataloguing Description*, Rajat, New Delhi.

Augur, Charles P. 1989. *Information Sources in Grey Literature.* London: Bowker-Saur.

Bliss, Henry E. (1910). A modern classification for libraries, with simple notation, mnemonics, and alternatives. *Library Journal* 35, 351–358.

Bliss, Henry E. (1935). *A system of bibliographic classification.* New York: H.W. Wilson.

Bliss, Henry E. (1940-1953). *A bibliographic classification, extended by systematic auxiliary schedules for composite specification* (4 volumes). New York: H.W. Wilson.

Burman, J.S., 2007. *Library Cataloguing: Principles and Practices,* Rajat, New Delhi.

Burman, J.S., 2009. *Recent Advances in Library Classification and Acquisition*, Rajat, New Delhi.

Carter, Mary Duncan, Wallace John Bank, and Rose Mary Magrill. 1974. *Building Library Collections*, 4th ed. Metuchen, N.J.:Scarecrow Press, Inc.

Chan, Lois Mai. *Cataloging and Classification: An Introduction.* New York: McGraw-Hill, 1994.

Chapman, Liz. 1989. *Buying Books for Libraries.* London: Library Association/Bingley.

DDC Dewey Decimal Classification : proposed revision of 780 music / prepared under the direction of Russell

Sweeney and John Clews with assistance from Winton E. Mathews, Jr. Albany N.Y. : Forest Press, 1980.

Debachere, M. C. *Problems in obtaining grey literature.* IFL4 Journal, 21(2) 1995, p. 94-98.

Evans, G. Edward. 1987. *Developing Library and Information Center Collections,* 2nd ed. Englewood Cliffs, CO.: Libraries Unlimited.

Gardener, Richard K. 1981. *Library Collections: Their Origin, Selection, and Development.* New York: McGraw-Hill.

Gorman, G.E. and B.R. Howes. 1989. *Collection Development for Libraries.* London: Centre for Information Studies.

Grieder, Theodore. 1978. *Acquisitions: Where, What, and How.* Westport, CT.: Greenwood Press, Inc.

Hill, Blaine H. 1985. *Collection Assessment Manual for College and University Libraries.* Phoenix: The Oryx Press.

Hirtle, Peter. 1991. *Broadsides vs. Grey Literature.*

Information World. 1996. *What is grey literature?*

Internet Archive: Details: The British Catalogue Of Music 1960.

Kabir, Abulfazal M. "Ranganathan: A Universal Librarian." *Journal of Educational Media and Library Sciences.* 40:4 (June 2003) :453-59.

Katz, William A. 1980. *Collection Development: The Selection of Materials for Libraries.* New York: Holt, Rinehart, and Winston.

Katz, William A. 1992. *Introduction to Reference Work Volume I: Basic Information Sources,* 6th ed. New York: McGraw-Hill.

Kumar, S., *Encyclopaedia of Library and Information Management* (2 vols.), Rajat, New Delhi, 2008.

Magrill, Rose Mary, and John Corbib. 1989. *Acquisitions Management and Collection Development in Libraries,* 2nd ed. Chicago: American Library Association.

Maltby, Arthur & Gill, Lindy (1979). *The case for Bliss.* London: Clive Bingley.

Morelon, Régis & Roshdi Rashed (1996), *Encyclopedia of the History of Arabic Science,* vol. 3, Routledge.

Ranganathan, Shiyali Ramamrita. "The Five Laws of Library and information Science", Delhi, Ess Ess Publications (Reprint) 2007.

Ranganathan, Shiyali Ramamrita. *The Five Laws of Library Science.* London: Edward Goldston. 1931.

Reed-Scott, Jutta. 1991. *Typology of selection sources.* Pp. 301-312 in Charles B. Osburn and Ross Atkinson (eds.) *Collection Management: A New Treatise.* London: JAI Press.

Rubin, Richard E. *Foundations of Library and Information Science.* 2nd ed. New York: Neal-Schuman Publishers. 2004.

Svenonius, Elaine. *The Intellectual Foundation of Information Organization.* Cambridge, Mass: MIT Press, 2000.

Thomas, Alan R. (1997). Bibliographical classification: the ideas and achievements of Henry E. Bliss. *Cataloging & Classification Quarterly* 25 (1), 51–104.

White, Herbert. 1984. *Managing the Special Library.* White Plains, N. Y.: Knowledge Industries Publications, Inc.

INDEX

■■■